forgotten HEROES

An American Soldier's Journey from Korea through the Cold War

1927-2016

EDWARD LEE SMITH

ISBN 978-1-950818-89-1 (paperback)

Rushmore Press LLC
1 888 733 9607
www.rushmorepress.com

Printed in the United States of America

CONTENTS

For all the brave men and women in the US military, and for America's cherished fallen. Your valor has not been forgotten.

**ALL WAR IS A SYMPTOM OF MAN'S FAILURE
AS A THINKING ANIMAL. —John Steinbeck**

AUTHOR'S NOTE

As I LISTEN TO THE news, my heart often breaks. It seems that gun violence is at an epidemic level, and the deadly contagion continues to spread far and wide. Shootings cut across all races, ethnicities, and economic levels. Anyone who loses a loved one to gun violence will weep, regardless of race or ethnicity. The proliferation of police shootings of young black men breaks my heart. The ambushing of police officers simply trying to do their jobs to protect and serve breaks my heart. Movements started by major activist organizations like Black Lives Matter and Moms Demand Action for Gun Sense in America seek to stop the bloodshed in America. Such movements give me hope that we, as Americans, can look beyond racial and ethnic hatred and instead love and understand one another.

Yes, we're all different. We're all individuals. We're just people, just Americans all in the same boat together, whether we like it or not. We are one nation under God, yet for some of us, it feels as if we're many unequal nations inside a bigger nation, rattling around like ball bearings thrown into a vicious blender. The balls hit the metal blades, chewing them up little by little, thereby eroding what we all stand for as a noble and brave people. The chewing sound is abrasive, even scary.

What we have going on here is scary. The economic inequality that also cuts across all races and ethnicities, the Congress that doesn't seem able to do a damn thing to help the people who pay its members, the stagnant wages, the denigration of unions, the demise of the pension, the constant threat to Social Security from those who wish to privatize it, the skyrocketing medical care costs, the complete disregard for others' lives as long as the individual is happy and sweet in his or her own life— these are all very scary to me. Frankly, they're un-American, and I don't like them one bit.

I'm a really old black guy. I'm proud of it. I can see we blacks are still fighting to get an even footing in America, and I don't like that either. We fight for our country. We die for our country. We work hard. We dream. We love. We have problems just like anybody else. Yet it's no secret that African Americans' average financial net worth is far less than white Americans'. It's no secret that young black men wind up in prison more often than their white counterparts. It's no secret that black-on-black gun violence in certain urban African American neighborhoods turns the streets into veritable war zones at night, when gangs are on the prowl and police are hesitant to even venture forth.

Inequality among the races, and that includes the Latino community from an ethnic point of view, does indeed exist in 2016. There's no denying it. And let's just leave religion out of it for now. That's a whole can of worms in itself, what with the rage against Muslims, which reminds me a lot of the indiscriminate rage against Japanese Americans during World War II, who got thrown into internment camps. If an evil leader sent military forces to bomb Pearl Harbor, did that mean all Japanese Americans were evil too? Let's not talk about excluding people based on race, religion, gender, or sexual orientation. Let's talk about including all Americans in what I see as an ongoing version of the American experiment that began in 1776, when we declared our independence against colonial rule from the British Empire.

As I was about to put this memoir to bed at last, I had the good fortune to celebrate my eighty-ninth birthday in nearly perfect health. I am forever grateful that everything seems to be working okay, including my brain. Old age is fun if you've got your health and your faculties and enough money to live on. Most of the good friends I've loved are gone, but that's the reality you face when you get old. As a veteran, I lived through the bloody combat in Korea during the counteroffensive of 1951, serving as a rifleman for the Seventh Infantry Division. We lost a lot of good guys, white and black. After I left active army duty, I immediately joined the National Guard and eventually worked my way up to lieutenant colonel. I commanded many great soldiers, white and black. For me, the military was a safe haven back in the days when being black in America was definitely no picnic. The ants showed up. I hate ants.

I grew up in North Carolina under the oppressive Jim Crow laws that pervaded the South. Lynching was more common than you might think. The Ku Klux Klan really did burn crosses on people's lawns and intimidated anyone who got in their way. The KKK made life unbearable for blacks unlucky enough to find themselves in their crosshairs. I suffered the direct consequences of racial discrimination quite often in those days. In 2016, some African Americans suffer from racial discrimination, but it's usually subtle. Blacks today don't have to go through special black entrances at stores, sit in segregated balconies in movie theaters, and drink from public water fountains designated For Colored Only.

Looking deep into my past as a black man in America, I can honestly say that we have made significant progress since the 1930s. The civil rights movement of the 1960s made a huge difference. Under Dr. Martin Luther King Jr.' s leadership, we all suddenly had a collective voice that got heard through nonviolent protests, which led to real change in America. Today, nonviolent movements can accomplish real change as well. I play a small part in spreading racial understanding to young kids when I speak about my experiences in high schools. The kids, white and black, are curious. They want to know about what I saw in North Carolina during the Great Depression, on the battlefields of Korea, and in the top-secret environs of the White Sands Missile Range in New Mexico. With curiosity come understanding and knowledge, and with those can come racial unity that will translate into a stronger and more peaceful United States of America.

So, even as my heart breaks when I listen to the news, I still have great hope for our country. We really can tear down the divides that separate us. It may not happen in my lifetime. In fact, I'm pretty sure it won't, because I'm a very old man. But it can happen if we all work together.

I know it will happen.

PREFACE

A MEMOIR IS BY ITS very nature a personal thing. It involves an individual sitting down with a piece of paper and a pen, or a computer. Either way, the paper or screen is blank before you start, much like in life when you become conscious of the world around you after emerging from the blissful no awareness of infancy. The blankness of an empty page can be quite daunting, as is the prospect of filling pages with bits and pieces of patched-together events, thoughts, emotions, insights, and revelations that go into filling up a full life, lived long and hard through the good and the bad times. The process of looking back requires introspection, a willingness to move into emotionally difficult and sometimes-dangerous terrain. Most memoirs remain locked in the vaults of would-be writers' heads, never to see the light of day. Others actually get written down in proper form and, if the author is lucky, even get read by complete strangers because the story is compelling.

When I set out to write about my life as an African American soldier and teacher in America during the tumultuous twentieth century, I had a very personal mission in mind. You might say I needed to face my demons. My twin brother, Fred, and I saw some of the bloodiest combat in the Korean War. We were both riflemen with the Seventh Infantry Division of the US Army. The fighting was intense. In fact, Fred and I were the only survivors in our company, solely due to luck. We lived not because we were brave but because we weren't in the wrong place at the wrong time. We happened to get sent home on compassionate leave because Grandma Jennie, the tough yet loving woman who raised us after our parents abandoned us at the start of the Great Depression, had suffered a massive heart attack and were on the brink of death. The same morning we shipped out of Korea to give solace to the family that took us in, more than two hundred men, our black and white brothers in arms, got wiped out in a horrifying assault by the North Koreans in the hilly no-man's-land along the now-notorious 38th parallel. If we'd been there ...

If ... What if? Why me? Why not Fred? Why were we spared when so many others weren't? When we served in King Company in 1951, we engaged in what historians now call the Battle of the Hills. It was a bloody, terrifying experience. The North Koreans and the Chinese tried to push us back to the Pusan Perimeter, a little nook of land in the lower portion of the Korean Peninsula. We'd been pushed back there before, and then, after Inchon, we pushed the enemy back almost to the meandering Yalu River on the Chinese border.

And then the Chinese got rather annoyed with the United Nations' forces and sent so many divisions across the border starting in October 1950 that we got pushed back again. And again. And again. Finally, when Fred and I showed up, the war was in a red-hot rage. Both sides were out for blood, and, golly, did each side tally up the dead. There were piles of dead Americans. Bodies blown to bits. Brains and guts spread out on gray rocks covered in red gore. Bullets, mortar shells, and incoming heavies from the big guns created a noise you can't imagine unless you've been there. The saddest thing of all is I can still hear the dying and wounded cries. When a shell lands right next to you and you think you're about to meet God, you're not really paying attention to the guy who's just gotten his leg blown off and is screaming, "Mama! Oh, God! Mama!" But when those periodic lulls come, and they always do in combat and in life, you can hear your buddies screaming, crying, and dying, and you wonder when your ticket will get punched. In life, you can sometimes hear yourself screaming too. Life isn't easy. Anyone who says it is just is a plain old idiot. Life is hard. Life is beautiful. Life is worth living.

So, for more than forty years, I thought about writing this story. I didn't do it until close to my eighty-ninth birthday because it was simply just too painful for me to go back to Korea, or to go back even earlier, to the days that shaped me and my brother as tough young black men, even though we didn't know growing up on a farm in North Carolina might just have saved our lives because it conditioned us for combat. Real tough. Real strong. Real mean and bad, as they sometimes say today. I questioned, *Why me? Why Fred? Why did I see so many of my brothers in arms die right next to me, and why did I get to live and they didn't?* Why does any life really matter? Aren't we all expendable? Aren't we just little ants running around with the collective purpose of the colony, or country, as the driving force that motivates us beyond the basics needed to survive? As I said, I hate ants. We're not ants. We're Americans!

I still don't have the answers. For a long time, I thought about calling this memoir *Why Me?* Ultimately, I chose a more Hollywood-friendly title, one that better captures the essence of one humble African American soldier's story. But I think the reason why I initially chose *Why Me?* stemmed from a lasting sense of survivor's guilt that has never quite called it quits, even so many years since I was at war in Korea. My brother is long dead. Almost everyone I knew back in the day is dead. I'm an old guy who lives on top of a mountain in New Mexico. I've got a great view— a stunning view. My best neighbor is an elk! The elk doesn't have parties with loud music that keep me up at night. The elk is quiet, stately, a creature of God. Human neighbors live far enough away that I never know whether they're home. If they have a party, I don't really care.

I think the spectacular view from my very own part of the Zuni Mountains has helped me get a better view into myself as a man, a Christian, a dad, a granddad, and a great-granddad. I see the way my maternal grandparents brought me up, in a strong Christian household, laid the foundation upon which I was able to build a life that actually meant something on a level that extended well beyond the ordinary. My second wife, Louise, introduced me to the Bahá'i faith, and that, too, has helped me find the inner peace I so longed for.

I think the so-called wisdom of the twilight of my life has also given me a vantage point from which I can look objectively at American society, both then and now, and reflect on it with a sober and discerning eye. Just look at what was happening when my brother and I were drafted in October 1950. We were two country boys caught up in an international bar fight, a Communism versus the West battle that started the Cold War, roared through Korea, and festered through Vietnam and beyond. As young black men, we were considered cannon fodder. Nobody really gave a damn if we were killed or not— except us, of course. The same thing happened in Vietnam. The same thing sometimes happens even now, especially on the streets of poor urban neighborhoods.

The war had gone badly for the United Nations' forces almost from the start, in 1950, when the Chinese responded to an America-led counteroffensive that threatened to drive the North Korean Army all the way to the Yalu River, on China's border. In response, the Chinese launched a major counteroffensive of their own in October that fired up with horrifying consequences for the First Marine Division at the Chosin Reservoir in November and December. American soldiers froze to death, nearly starved in the field, and bravely repelled the overwhelming Chinese onslaught during the withdrawal to the south. Fred and I weren't in Korea yet, but the battles after we got there just got worse and worse as the Chinese and North Koreans drove south to pursue the UN coalition. Even at the age of eighty-eight, I still sometimes have nightmares. I still vividly recall the carnage. Sometimes, a whiff of cold air, a certain unpleasant smell, or the crack of a backfire can trigger a flashback. I can tell you one thing: I'm not a big fan of fireworks.

As I said, a soldier never forgets. But the memories do fade and become less of a burden with the passage of time. That's just the way of things. The human mind adjusts, if you're in luck. Yet my wartime experiences caused me to stay somewhat distant from those I loved and those who loved me. I had some anger issues, not only because of the war but also because of the prejudice shown to me as a black man for decades, both in and out of the army. I also stayed angry with my parents for abandoning Fred and me when we were barely three years old.

In June 2012, Louise left me after twenty-five years of marriage, and I haven't dated a woman since. I was eighty-five at the time. She didn't leave me solely because of my demons, but the ghosts I still carried with me did play a part in our separation and subsequent divorce. I went into therapy after that. I realized I had to face the darkest parts of my life with the same courage I summoned when my rifle squad faced the North Koreans and the Chinese. It was during my therapy sessions that my decision to actually write this memoir solidified and became tangible. As I said, I'd toyed with writing about my life experiences for nearly forty years, but I never followed through. Now, I was determined to get the process going, regardless of how painful it was.

And it was painful. A soldier isn't a machine. A soldier is a human being forced into a situation nobody should have to experience. A soldier is the sum of his or her life, those events that came before and worked to shape the individual. For me, my journey as a soldier began almost immediately after my birth in 1927. The times were tough enough for an African American family in Philadelphia, where I was born. They got even tougher when the stock market crashed in 1929. The crucible of poverty and the emotional damage that occurred after my parents abandoned my brother and me left indelible impressions on my mind, as if a force of nature had scoured my soul bare like a desert wind that sandblasts the flesh until it cracks and bleeds. When I wrote about my early days, I often found myself weeping. When I wrote about Korea, I had to think about things I'd just as soon forget.

So, an old soldier's memoir will, by necessity, have more than war to talk about. It will hold a life's essence. Another reason why I chose to write this book is that I wanted to share my experiences with future generations of my family, and with present loved ones who might desire further insight into their dad, granddaddy, or great-grandpa. I also wanted to honor my beloved twin brother, Fred; may he rest in peace. At the age of eighty-eight, and as the last living member of my immediate family, I'm slowing down a bit, which shouldn't be a real big surprise to anyone. I don't know when I'll be called home to my final peace, so I figured I'd best get started with the writing before it was too late!

As I began writing, I had to face myself in ways I had not done before. That's a point that bears repeating. Even a man of courage, in the fog of war in the blood-soaked crags of mountainous North Korea, can shy away from the hard truths. He can fight the enemy, but if the enemy is himself, the battle is harder to win. A man lost in the daily grind of life can lose sight of his true self and of what's really important. The soldier and the civilian can both fail to stand long enough in front of a mirror to see the full meaning that lies in the depths of his eyes, in the creases that time has eroded in his cheeks and forehead.

It's easy to run away. It's easy to blame others. It's easy to stick your head in the sand and pretend your life could have turned out differently if it weren't for something someone else did to stop you from pursuing your dreams. I had to look hard at where I went wrong and what I'd done right. I had to look at the very real obstacles that were thrown my way, or that I put up myself. I grew up during the Great Depression on my maternal grandfather's farm in Northampton County, North Carolina. It was a hard life, but we were actually better off than many African Americans in inland North Carolina. We at least had food to eat and a house to live in. The Depression nevertheless left a lasting impression on me. As for many of us who lived through it, those times changed and shaped our lives. My grandfather and grandmother's strict nature also left a lasting impression. We weren't allowed to express our feelings. We weren't allowed to cry. We had to be strong and bear our individual sufferings in complete silence.

The writing process was difficult because it made me look deep into myself. Sometimes, I liked what I saw, and sometimes, I didn't. It also made me look at my country with the perspective of nearly nine decades of life, and like with myself, sometimes, I liked what I saw, and sometimes, I didn't. So, in a way, my story is America's story, at least in regard to the twentieth century. It reflects the long passage we African Americans have made and have still yet to make. It reflects the evolution of society as a whole. I, for one, could hardly have imagined that I'd live to see the day when a black man could win a presidential election and take up residence in the White House as the leader of the most powerful country in the world. But Barack Obama did just that. Twice.

I've tried to live my life with the guiding belief that extra effort counts. If you go the whole nine yards, plus a few more for extra measure, you'll eventually get where you want to end up. When I retired as a lieutenant colonel after more than two decades of service to my country on active army duty, as well as a long stint afterward in the National Guard, I had been a teacher of high school and college students since the mid-1960s. I told my students that putting extra effort into all aspects of life takes guts and tenacity, but it's necessary if you want to get ahead. As minorities, we have to put in extra effort to excel in a society that sometimes holds us back, even today. Some of my students thought I was a fool; others didn't. If you can keep smiling when life gets you down, you'll realize that you can overcome what you face. That's what I've known all along. It's just sometimes hard to keep that belief in mind. If you can hold true to yourself most of the time, then I think you'll make out just fine. I know I have, through thick and thin.

PROLOGUE

I CROUCHED LOW IN A natural rock ditch eroded into a man-size grave carved out over millennia of frozen winters and rain-soaked springs in the high mountains of North Korea. I clutched my M1 Garand semiautomatic rifle tight. Ammo was low, but I had enough eight-round clips loaded with .30-caliber Springfield slugs to take on whatever came my way. I felt sure we'd be in the thick of combat again at any moment.

I led First Squad, still miraculously at full strength, with twelve men, after we received replacements to fill the ranks thinned in previous combat. I was forward of the main front line in my part of the grid, where the three other squads in my platoon similarly dug in. I was alone in my rock nook, keeping a watchful eye out for any surprises the North Koreans might have planned for my guys. All along the boulders and crannies halfway up the slope before me, my buddies in King Company were fanned out. Altogether, we were some 235 men strong. The number varied by a dozen or more every day as the dead and wounded were tallied and the replacements, many of whom had never even fired an M1 before, were sent forward to keep us at full combat strength.

Above me, up the rocky grade, was yet another nondescript hill looming large, sharp, gray, and deadly in the early morning mist. As usual, we'd moved forward to push on the enemy line. The hill we were on was on that constantly moving line, right in the face of our very effective North Korean and Chinese adversaries. We had to take that hill, no matter the cost in American blood. I knew some of my men would die in a matter of minutes or hours. I cared about that. But I didn't grieve over it. The horror and terror of it all had stopped impacting me as it once had when I was first on the line. It all got deep inside me like some sort of horrid tapeworm. I no longer trembled when I heard the whoosh of incoming heavy artillery rounds and one of my men screamed, "Incoming!" I just instinctively knew to get my head down, and get it down fast, to avoid the rainstorm of hot shrapnel, bits of razor rock, and splinters of dead wood from any tree left standing like a blackened skeleton, seeming to beckon my soul to either come to Jesus or join hands with the devil.

Enemy small-arms fire remained intermittent, but I knew that wouldn't last. Yet, for the moment, neither side was in a big hurry to get to the killing. The North Korean troops held the high ground, always an advantage in battle because you get to shoot down on the enemy while your foe has to shoot up. When you're running up a hill with bullets flying all around you, you present an excellent target. When you hold the high ground, it's the enemy who has a bull's-eye painted at center mass. I hadn't been in combat all that long. However, I'd already learned my war lessons well. I'd seen too many of my brothers in arms fall, the dead and dying littering the craggy hills of a country I hadn't known existed prior to the outbreak of the so-called police action in Korea on June 25, 1950. T saw seventy-five thousand soldiers from the North Korean People's Army swarm the 38th parallel to the south, going into the pro-Western Republic of Korea.

The enemy knew where we were and that we'd be stupid enough to charge up that stinking hill. I wondered where my twin brother, Fred, was. We were both privates, and we both led squads in King Company. Fred led the 4th Squad. I hoped he was okay. I hoped he would still be okay when the sun went down.

Fred and I had been assigned to the Seventh Infantry Division after going through our basic training at Fort Dix, an army base in New Jersey, and our subsequent field training in Korea with an all-black army ranger unit. The segregated unit ran contrary to Harry S. Truman's executive order in 1948, demanding that the US military integrate its forces, but the army changed slowly. Many of our commanding officers apparently didn't get Truman's memo. The rangers had taken us under their protective wings and showed us the ropes so that we newbie combat troops might live through our first firefight. Now, out on this desolate, mortar-scarred hill, we black troops truly were fighting alongside our white brethren. When we got replacements to fill in the ranks after taking heavy casualties, race didn't matter. A soldiers' specialty with weapons counted most. If we needed a machine gunner, our CO didn't give a rat's ass if the guy was black or white. The guy just had to know how to shoot straight when a bunch of the enemy tried to take him out as quickly as possible.

The Seventh Infantry Division had taken it on the chin since it landed in Korea in September 1950. That November, the Chinese crossed the Yalu River and slammed into the United Nations' forces with twelve divisions. The bastards decimated much of our division. Things didn't go any better at the Chosin Reservoir, where we lost three whole battalions in a bloodbath that racked up two thousand casualties in just those three units. The First Marine Division got it even worse. Fred, who also served as a rifleman in King Company, and I missed all the early action, but we were in the soup at that point, for sure. The war was just a little less than one year old, and it felt like an eternity to all us GI Joes who'd been drafted and forced into arms.

I eased my head up over the lip of the little ditch, nudging my helmet up just enough so I could see and not expose too much of my head to snipers. All was strangely quiet, except for the occasional crack of a rifle in the distance, or the rumble of artillery even farther away. An American fighter jet roared by, giving me an odd and stupid sense of security. I always hated those moments before our platoon leader, a white, wet-behind-the-ears second lieutenant West Point graduate, gave the order to advance. I felt the enemy's eyes on me. My skin crawled. My heart raced enough for me to hear it thumping in my ears.

Where are you, Fred? I wondered. Keep your damned head down. Keep it down! You hear me, brother?

1 SNOWFALL

THE SUN WASN'T UP AT 0530, but I could still see the snow clotted on the two immense alligator junipers in my yard, which have been there for more than one thousand years. Smaller junipers, redwoods, and pinyon trees were similarly adorned in white. My house, the beautiful three-bedroom my second ex-wife, Louise, and I purchased back in 1997, was a bit chilly. It was a retreat for us, ensconced in the Zuni Mountains in southwestern New Mexico between the big cities of Albuquerque and Gallup at an altitude of more than eight thousand feet. We'd lived there together for fifteen years before our marriage ended in June 2012, just before my eighty-sixth birthday in July. For me, the place was—and still is—almost sacred, like a church of nature, my own fifteen-acre slice of heaven where I live alone with my dog and spend much time contemplating my life's path. I padded into the kitchen, Molly anxious to get outside to do her business.

"Okay, you silly fussbudget," I said to Molly as I went to the door. "I know you would rather be outside. See! See! It's snowed! Look at the pretty snow!"

Molly barked. She likes barking. Perhaps a bit too much.

I laughed. "It's gonna be cold out there, you know!"

A mutt of no certain breed with a light brown coat, Molly is a companion in my mostly solitary world in the mountains. She is difficult sometimes because she is the consummate escape artist, always looking for a way under the fence I built for her. If she escaped and I couldn't find her, odds are good that a mountain lion would. She is the epitome of an "outside dog," as they say in the Southeast.

I let Molly out and breathed in the frosty April air. It was invigorating, life-affirming, and also cold enough for me to close the door with a shiver. Before I did, I hesitated just long enough to watch snowflakes illuminated in the soft light of the lanterns I'd installed on the deck my son Gil and I built together three years earlier. My house on Zuni Canyon Road is miles from anywhere, which was how I liked it when I bought it with Louise, and it's how I like it now. Gil lives thirty miles away in the city of Grants, but I see him often just the same. Of my six children from two wives, geographically, he is the closest to me.

Ready for some coffee and a light breakfast, usually oatmeal, I loaded up the filter, poured water into the percolator, and hit the switch. The sound of the coffee machine always reminds me of breathing. The next order of business was to fire up my wood-burning stove. The house has no fireplace, so the stove is a comfort, especially on cold days. Soon, the fire's crackle merged with the rhythmic melody of fresh coffee brewing. The smell of the coffee filled the kitchen with a tantalizing fragrance, which always makes me feel at home. The first light of dawn, gray and indistinct, colored the big windows that afford me a panoramic, 270-degree view of the forest. One of my favorite times of day is dawn, when the world seems full of promise and life renews itself in the cycle of another day born. I went into the den and flipped on my satellite TV, already tuned to the local classical music station. To my delight, Nicolai Rimsky-Korsakov's *Scheherazade / Capriccio Espagnol* was playing. His Russian Easter Overture is grand in all its dimensions.

Seated at the kitchen table after filling my coffee mug, I simply watched the gray light fill the windows while I ate my oatmeal after it had sat a bit to set, but not long enough for it to take on the consistency of glue made from an old horse. On the table sat a three-ring loose-leaf binder, like the kind kids use in elementary school. I'd bought stacks of white paper with three holes already punched in them to fill the binder. The pages in the binder were covered in words from my soul, legibly written in black ink, the well-formed letters of each word filling the space between the thin blue lines. For months, I'd sat in my kitchen writing down the events of my life, driven to exorcise the ghosts that had resided deep inside me since I was a little boy.

I leaned back in my chair, yawned, and stretched my arms out in front of me. The Zuni Mountains slowly became visible through the windows. The snow still fell, but it was no blizzard, merely a late-spring snowstorm ushered in on the heels of a west wind laden with moisture from the vast Pacific Ocean. At that moment, all seemed right with the world, even though the larger world was in its usual mess, with terrorists, political gridlock, racial and ethnic strife, gun violence, and global financial jitters, as the Chinese economic locomotive appeared to have lost steam. The UK had just voted to leave the European Union. The larger world seemed to be going to hell in a hand basket.

I had at last finished writing the story of my life. I felt an immeasurable sense of peace, contentment, and self-satisfaction.

The process hadn't been easy. In fact, the prospect of confronting my ghosts had kept me away from paper and pen for nearly forty years—I don't have a computer; don't need one. I don't need e-mail or Facebook. I don't even need a typewriter. My one acquiescence to technology is my satellite TV. And I have an ancient cell phone I intend to trash in the near future; I have no intention whatsoever of replacing it. When you think of it, that's pretty ironic, considering I mastered software development and analysis when computers were the size of rooms and a real-life bug could actually gum up the works if one crawled inside the mainframe. The lack of technology in my later years is even more ironic when you consider I started one of the first black-owned and -operated software development businesses in the United States, long before Microsoft and Apple were hot stocks, but that brief entrepreneurial foray occurred a long time ago; it ended up bust.

It has indeed been a long run—my life, I mean. That is for sure. Not many Americans live as long as I have. At the ripe old age of eighty-eight during the writing of this story, I'd seen my share of living. In Korea with the Seventh Infantry Division, I'd seen my share of dying. On the battlefield, bullets and shrapnel don't care if you're black or white, yellow, or brown. The hot metal and splintered stone kill and maim no matter what color you are. As an African American of my advanced age, I've lived through Jim Crow, the Ku Klux Klan, war, the civil rights movement, economic booms and busts, the birth of rock 'n' roll, the free love and drugs of the 1960s, the assassination of Martin Luther King Jr., the women's liberation movement, the tech bubble, and the Great Recession, which cost millions of Americans whatever money they'd managed to save for retirement. As I sat looking up from the three-ring binder to the view outside, just thinking about it all made my head spin. Yet there it all was—written down, captured like a will-o'-the-wisp in an all-too-real fairy tale.

Time is precious, yet I'd wasted so much of mine. I'd lived, loved, and lost, like all of us. But there never seemed to be enough time. There still isn't. I know it. A person's life doesn't rewind like a watch or self-regenerate on solar power. It is more like an hourglass with a finite amount of sand to run through to the pile gathering steadily in the lower half. I sat there thinking about that for a few long moments, and then I got up from my chair to stretch my legs and get Molly back inside, if she'd let me. A Beethoven sonata playing on the TV ended. The host of the show broke for the newscast. I rested my backside against the counter.

"Do you really want to hear the news?" I said as I rinsed my coffee mug in the sink.

I thought better of fogging my thoughts with news, which was bound to be all bad, all doom and gloom. But I stopped when word said that a possible bout of severe wintry weather was on its way, morphing the gentle snowstorm into something a little more serious. I glanced out the windows. The snow fell at the same rate. The sun was just nudging over the peaks to the east, masked by the dense cloud cover. Conditions didn't look threatening just then, but I knew that the weather could change in the blink of an eye high up in the mountains. I walked outside onto the deck, the spring of youth long gone from my step. I was careful not to slip and fall. Living alone so far from the nearest medical facilities, I could experience dire consequences if I broke one of my old, creaky bones.

When people meet me for the first time, most think I'm about twenty years younger. My eyesight still functions, though I wear glasses. My hair went MIA long ago, leaving me with a pleasant brown dome to top off my lanky frame. My brain processes thoughts and feelings sometimes far too well, and while I do have an occasional "senior moment," I'm doing pretty nicely on the cognitive front. Perhaps my longevity is due to good genes. Maybe it's because I never drank alcohol to excess. I've never been drunk in my life, something that really amazes some people. I've had visitors who marvel at the surroundings of my Zuni retreat. They literally gush and ooh and ah, until they find out I don't like to keep alcohol in the house. The lack of alcohol detracts from what should be a pure experience of nature's grandeur. Visitors like that don't often come back to see me again, and I guess that's all for the best, however sad it may be. And, for the record, I've also never smoked, not even in Korea. I'd give away the cigarettes issued with our rations, making me a very popular guy.

"Molly!"

I glanced around. Where are you, you little mutt? I thought. Ah, there you are! I saw a brown patch of fur set against the newly fallen layer of snow in the yard. The patch moved; then it barked. Molly glanced over her shoulder at me, giving me a look—I swore it was one of disdain—and turned back to whatever she found so interesting near the fence. A deer emerged from the dense stand of trees on the other side of the yard. I watched it stand stock still, as if doing so would make it invisible to me. Molly caught the deer's scent and ran across the yard, barking and spooking the tawny creature.

"Come on, Molly! It's freezing out here! Come here, girl! Come on."

Molly was having none of it. I sighed. I stalked back inside, put on my boots and coat, and went out to collect my stubborn little mutt. Once we were both back inside, I warmed my hands by the stove. I thought about my story. I was going to read it over to see if I'd actually achieved what I'd set out to do. A person can try to achieve a goal, but it doesn't mean success is guaranteed. On the contrary, failure is often more frequent than success. Yet I've always felt that the worst thing a person can do is fail to try, not try and fail.

My childhood in rural North Carolina during the Great Depression, and my relatively happy teen years during World War II, flashed through my mind like a movie. The film continued as I once again keenly felt a tinge of bitterness at my mostly thwarted desire to find financial and emotional success during the postwar years, when racial discrimination against blacks remained undiminished despite the fact that approximately one million black men served their nation—though, with few exceptions, they served in segregated noncombat support units, not on the front lines with their white counterparts. My combat years in Korea also stirred in my mind like a dangerous, big cat hungry for blood.

I thought about my subsequent years in the army, smiling and shaking my head at some of the funny stories and applying the balm of late-life wisdom to soothe the blisters of still more racial discrimination as I rose up in the ranks of the US Army and National Guard to finally retire as a lieutenant colonel. One of my more interesting duty stations found me working at the White Sands Missile Range doing top-secret research on missile technology. It was the height of the Cold War. It was a sad and scary time when kids practiced duck-and-cover nuclear attack drills in school and when people dug bomb shelters in their backyards.

So much has changed in my life. Divorce. New love. Love lost again. Another divorce. The births of my six kids, the arrivals of precious grandchildren, and the evolution of my teaching career after leaving active duty in the army. If I've learned anything over the long years I've lived, it is that change is as inevitable as the sun rising.

In my increasingly pensive mood, as I stood in front of my wood-burning stove, I considered chapter 2 of my life, a chapter of learning and teaching. I am an educated man. I speak five languages: English, Japanese, Spanish, French, and the language of the dominant tribe in Liberia. I'm proud of that. Very few Americans are even bilingual. In chapter 2 of my existence on this mortal coil, I dedicated my career to helping disadvantaged students overcome the obstacles that keep them from a chance to better themselves. I did this in the United States, and in Liberia during a two-year stint in the Peace Corps. Without an education, doors to success and prosperity will likely stay closed, which is why I lament the disparity between poor and wealthy school districts, not only in the black community but in the white, Latino, and Asian communities as well. Still, for all my education and training, I've never been much of a philosopher. Perhaps writing the memoir changed that a little, or perhaps it helped me see who I really am for the first time. It let me look back through the years to see what shaped me as the man I've become.

They say you don't remember much of when you're one or two years old, but that is where my story begins. I agree that human beings don't have the capacity to travel back to a time in their lives when the world was so new and strange that no conscious vestiges of the experience linger within mental grasp. I certainly don't remember the day my twin brother, Fred, and I were born way back on July 3, 1927, in Philadelphia, Pennsylvania. I don't suppose anyone remembers being born on a conscious level, but I truly believe we all must carry some trace memories buried deep inside our brains.

I don't remember my mother or father, but not because they both died in a tragic car accident before we came of conscious age. I don't remember them because they abandoned my brother and me at the onset of the Great Depression, after the stock market crashed in 1929 and banks went bust all across the country. Fred and I didn't see our dad again until we were both thirteen years old. We never did know our mom. She evidently didn't care to know us. Later, when Fred and I were both young boys, we were told that she'd come to North Carolina to see her boyfriends. We'd ask why she didn't come see us.

"Oh, I suppose she likes her men friends better. She's a no-good tramp, your mama."

That's a hard thing for any kid to hear about his mom, even if it might be true. Despite my recent therapy after my divorce from Louise, the hurt remains. I doubt I'll ever get rid of it entirely. Perhaps some tenacious ghosts are meant to stay with you until you draw your last feeble breath.

I sighed and stopped rubbing my hands by the stove. I opened the door to the black hot belly and fed the fire inside with more fuel. The kitchen was warm and cozy. Full daylight had come. I could clearly see the snow-capped, craggy, volcanic peaks of the distant mountains rise above the snow-clad forest. Below, the valley stretched out before me in subdued splendor. Molly rested with her head nestled on her paws. I poured another cup of coffee and sat down to read what I'd spent so much time writing down, walking dark and light paths along the way to completing my task. I put on my glasses and opened the binder. When I picked up my mug to take a sip of coffee, I noticed that my hands were shaking. I began to read.

RESCUE

IN 1927, PHILADELPHIA TENEMENTS WERE much the same for poor blacks and whites. The brick low-rise buildings that lined the dingy streets had no hot running water. In winter, radiators rattled with steam, if the boilers worked. Icy drafts filtered through dilapidated window frames. In summer, people slept on the fire escapes to find relief from the heat and humidity. Despite their poverty, many tenants mostly took pride in their humble homes, even cleaning the stoops and sweeping the sidewalks. Just because a person is poor doesn't mean he or she lacks all dignity or humanity. Nobody wants to be poor; people just are, often through no fault of their own. Rather, they are poor because of circumstances beyond their control. Certainly some are poor because they fail to rise to meet challenges. They make the wrong choices time after time, or they lose themselves in the inertia of utter despair. Nothing is black or white when it comes to poverty; it's all pale shades of gray.

The tenements were that way. There were modicums of happiness and depths of grief, rage, and agony. It's human nature to carry on even in the cold face of desperate hardship. Amid the crime and squalor, boys played stickball. Girls jumped rope or played hopscotch. Fathers went to work in factories along the Delaware River, at construction sites, or wherever else an unskilled, uneducated man could find work. Mothers cared for crying babies, cooked meals, cleaned the apartments, and did the laundry. Mothers, boys, and girls worked in sweatshops for pennies to help the fathers make ends meet.

As was the case in most of the United States, African Americans lived in segregated neighborhoods. In the North, segregation wasn't mandatory, but blacks and whites kept apart anyway just because that's all anyone knew. It felt natural to stay separate, for blacks and whites alike. In the South, Jim Crow laws enacted after Reconstruction in the post–Civil War era made it a crime for blacks and whites to live together. Those state and local laws weren't repealed until 1965, at the height of the civil rights movement almost a century later. The longevity of Jim Crow stands as sad evidence of how racism was (and still is) stitched into the very fabric of American society.

My parents, Melinda Wall and Exum Smith, lived in Philly, trying to cope with their own troubles. My father liked the bottle— no, loved the bottle—which probably explains why I've never been a big fan of alcohol. My mother evidently loved men way too much for her own good. Of course, I don't remember this time of my life. Fred and I were just babies. I do know that neither parent wanted us. They were both too wrapped up in their own struggles, their own selfish desires, to care about twin boys deemed more of an inconvenience and a hardship than a blessing. Nevertheless, they kept us, fed us, and clothed us during those last years of the Roaring Twenties, a time of flappers, Prohibition, machine-gun-toting gangsters, and rampant speculation in the stock market. The wealthier class in America was doing fabulously well, but income inequality was every bit as present then as it is today across the entire American spectrum, regardless of race. My parents resided at the bottom of the heap.

I can only imagine how it came to be that my paternal grandmother, Ellen Smith, came to collect us from Philly to take us down to a tiny rural community not far from Roanoke Rapids, in inland northeastern North Carolina. Most likely, my dad wrote her a letter, saying my mom had run off with another man again and that he couldn't take care of us, or wouldn't. I do know the Depression was in full force. Millions of Americans, black and white, were financially ruined, jobless, and starving. I don't know how Grandma Ellen even got to Philly. She was living in poverty herself. She certainly didn't own a Model T. I doubt she even had money to buy a train ticket once she got herself to the closest station. In fact, she had nowhere to live, yet she came to get us. Somehow, she got all the way up to Philly because she knew her grandchildren needed her.

"You got to take 'em, Mama," my dad may have said when Grandma Ellen arrived at the tenement house. "I can't take care of 'em no more. Melinda's up and gone again. I got no job. They's hungry, Mama. The boys got to eat somethin'."

Grandma Ellen probably looked at her son with angry eyes that were simultaneously full of sadness. "You drunk, Exum. As usual."

"No, I ain't."

"Oh, yeah, you is! You spent less on the liquor, you'd have victuals for your young'uns. Where'd you git the money for that shine, anyways? Huh? Where'd you git it?"

Fred and I were probably clothed in rags, dirty, and very thin. We probably stared at our grandma with deep brown eyes, our innocence still unsullied by the cold and often-vicious ways of the world. No doubt my brother and I stood close together, drawing strength from each other. We shared an uncommon bond, as most twins do.

"I got no money to raise kids, Mama."

"But you got money for drink."

"Not no more. I don't got money no more."

"And you think I do? What you think I'm gonna do with two little babies? You hear? What you think I'm gonna do?"

"If you don't take 'em, I'll give 'em away to the church or the orphanage."

"You got a stone for a heart, boy."

However the confrontation went, it must not have been pleasant for Grandma Ellen. Her daughter-in-law's family, the Walls, also from northeastern North Carolina, had never liked the Smith family. I suspect they thought their daughter married the wrong guy, and they were probably right. But my mom was no sweetheart either, so I guess it took two to tango, as far as the family estrangement and mutual antipathy went. The thing is my maternal grandparents were in a much better place financially to take care of us than Grandma Ellen was, but they weren't even made aware of what was happening in Philly. As far as they knew, everything was okay, as much as that could be true, given the ravages of the Depression.

"Well, then," Grandma Ellen might have said, "I guess that's it. I'll take them babies because they cain't live here. Not with you anyways."

"Thanks, Mama."

"Don't thank me, boy. You oughta be ashamed of yourself. The good Lord is lookin' down on you right now and shakin' his ol' head. You a sinner, Exum. You a sinner, and God forgive you for what you doin' to your sweet babies."

Grandma Ellen bundled us up and took us away. My brother and I would one day return to the City of Brotherly Love, to bustling, urban Philly. But we had to grow up first, and we did our growing up far from breadlines; the New Deal; the Works Progress Administration, with its far-reaching jobs programs; and the more sophisticated trappings of city life. Instead, we landed in a rural state where Jim Crow reigned supreme. The Tar Heel State occupies many different geographic areas, stretching from the coastal lowlands all the way to the Appalachian Mountains to the west. Grandma Ellen took us to the Piedmont region, where you'll find hills and fields before the terrain begins to rise at the foothills. The land is rich and fertile for growing cotton, peanuts, soybeans, corn, and other crops. Sharecropping was the norm for poor blacks and whites living on expansive farms located miles from the nearest small town. In certain areas, though, black and white farmers owned their own land and worked it themselves, with the occasional hand from a neighbor if extra help was required during planting or harvest time.

Having to care for Fred and me must have been hard on Grandma Ellen. With no place of her own, she relied on the kindness of friends to put us up. In a way, it was like what happens today. One or both parents cannot take care of their kids, often due to a substance abuse problem, so a grandparent takes in the grandchildren, sparing them from the revolving door of the foster care system. Parents who have lost their jobs trek with their kids from one temporary safe haven to the next, until everyone they know no longer wants to see their faces at the front door. Eventually, the family ends up on the street or in a homeless shelter with little hope for the future. That was our life as Fred and I grew old enough to understand that we were not wanted anywhere, that our parents had turned us out into the cold, and that we didn't have enough to eat as Grandma Ellen doggedly made her way to the tar-paper shack of one friend or acquaintance after another, begging for food and a place for us to sleep for the night.

One of my earliest memories is burned into my mind. When adults were elsewhere in a shack we stayed in, most likely outside, Fred and I sneaked into the kitchen. In the flickering light of a kerosene lamp, we got down on our hands and knees, our faces inches from the dirty wooden floor.

"You see anythin', Fred?" I asked. I continued to crawl around, searching everywhere for a biscuit crumb, a squished piece of potato or onion, or a festering lump of pork fat. The grown-ups sometimes dropped food if they weren't paying attention, and we wanted to eat their scraps.

"Nope. Don't see nothin'."

"Keep lookin'. There's got to be somethin' here to eat."

The problem was the grown-ups Grandma Ellen took us to stay with were starving too. Few of them were sharecroppers, who at least could grow their own food. Others caught fish in the creeks or foraged in the dense pine forests that hemmed in the fields, towns, and roads. Still others hunted for rabbits, squirrels, chipmunks, deer, and other game. But there was never enough for us to eat. Hunger is a terrible thing. If you're really hungry, you begin to feel dizzy and weak. You can't think straight because your brain is deprived of sufficient protein to carry out its basic functions. You entirely focus on finding food. It becomes an obsession because you know you're slowly dying. Your body is literally eating itself, starting with the fat and moving on to the muscle tissue.

For a boy of three or four, the pain of an empty stomach comes as a shock. I wondered what was happening to Fred and me. I wondered what we'd done that was so bad our parents left us to suffer. I just wanted it all to stop. But it didn't stop. The nomadic trudge through the countryside continued. Sometimes, we'd hitch a ride to the next possible haven in the back of a mule-drawn cart, but we mostly walked. Grandma Ellen became quiet. I think her life's hunger and pain had beaten her down to the point where she started to simply give up. It has been said that the first two or three years of your life play an immensely important part in shaping who you become as a person. If that is the case, then our time with Grandma Ellen must've taught Fred and me that we brothers had to look out for each other because nobody else seemed up to the job.

Then our dire situation came to the attention of our maternal grandparents, Jennie and William Wall, when an acquaintance of theirs visited them one Sunday after church. Years later, Fred and I were told what happened next.

"I hear tell that things are bad with your grandchildren," the visitor said.

"What do you mean? Things are bad all over," Grandpa William said. "We're in the middle of a dang depression."

The visitor explained that we were with our paternal grandmother, Ellen Smith. That came as a surprise to both Grandma

Jennie and Grandpa William. I know now that they were also pretty angry with Grandma Ellen. As I said, there was no love lost between the Walls and the Smiths. They'd been feuding for years, possibly decades.

"Why, I thought the boys were with our daughter Melinda up in Philadelphia!" Grandma Jennie said. "What in the Lord's name are they doing down here?"

"Couldn't say," the visitor said, "but Fred and Ed are definitely here with Miss Ellen. They look like they're ailin'. They're as skinny as sticks, their clothes are all tore up and dirty, and it looks like they haven't had a bath in months. Ellen don't look too good neither. Just thought y'all should know."

Grandpa William was not a man to be trifled with. He owned a farm in Northampton County with 168 acres of land around the farmhouse. He did not sharecrop the land, but worked it himself and sold the crops to local buyers. He was a wealthy man, compared to most in the vicinity of Rich Square, the nearest town to the farm. He and his family had built up the landholdings over the years, and the Walls had managed their finances well. They didn't believe in banks. They believed in hard work and cash money on the barrelhead when they made deals for their crops or beef cattle. Not every black man in North Carolina ended up broke during the Depression. In fact, there were enclaves of relatively prosperous black merchants and farmers. You just had to have a good pair of field glasses to find them.

The following Sunday, Grandpa William sent his son and eldest daughter to fetch us. He'd already gotten word to Grandma Ellen that he would take us in. She'd done everything she could, but I know she felt relieved to have the burden of our care finally off her shoulders. The Wall boy, my uncle, who was a strapping young man strong from years of work on the farm, arrived with my aunt in a mule-drawn wagon. A cold rain fell as Fred and I said good-bye to Grandma Ellen. We didn't have any possessions. We had a whole lot of nothing. We climbed into the back of the wagon, my uncle flipped the reins, and we were off.

Although my memory is foggy, what with these events taking place about eighty-six years ago, I do recall feeling displaced and scared. I'd never known Grandpa William, Grandma Jennie, my uncle and aunts, or anybody else outside of Grandma Ellen, my mom, and my dad. I'm reasonably sure that Fred felt the same way. Everything was strange and unknown as the wagon jolted and bumped along the unpaved country road. We had no coats. Our shoes were falling apart. We were so hungry, oh so hungry. As the rain picked up, so did the wind. The sky was gunmetal gray above the swaying pines. My uncle and aunt talked and cussed up front, urging the stubborn and weary mule to get going.

"We don't got all day!" shouted my uncle. He flipped the reins. The mule brayed in defiance.

The rain came down harder, making the bumpy, soggy, twenty-mile journey even more cold and miserable. When the wagon reached a creek, the water boiled and churned, scaring the mule. My fear increased. I'd never been on a ride like this. The Walls shouted and cursed, but they finally got the mule to obey and cross the creek. Sheets of wind-driven rain soaked us all to the skin.

Darkness had come by the time we arrived at Grandpa William's farm. There was no light near the barn, but my aunt lit a kerosene lamp. We watched as my aunt and uncle unhitched the mules, walked them to stalls, and gave them some hay to eat.

"Come on, now," my aunt said, "let's get you two into the house to warm up and have somethin' to eat. Mama's probably fretting something fierce by now."

We trudged through the mud toward the little farmhouse. In the window, I saw the faintest glow of a lamp. As I think back on that cold, damp night in the very dawn of my ability to recollect, I realize now that light was like a beacon for me, every bit as lifesaving as a lighthouse is for a ship seeking safe harbor in a terrible storm. I didn't know it at the time, of course. At the time, Fred and I were just two scared little boys cast adrift in a sea of the unknown during the turmoil and agony of the Great Depression.

CALLUSES

I TOOK A DEEP BREATH and looked away from the page in the binder. The tears had come, not in torrential sobs but as a warm, gentle trickle down my cheeks, like a summer rain. I quickly ran the back of my right hand across my face. I merely succeeded in spreading the tears around.

You old softy, I thought. You fight in a war. You see your buddies die in front of you, and you go waterworks over your messed-up childhood. What a chicken.

Soldiers aren't supposed to cry. Real men aren't supposed to show emotion. Bad guys are big and bad. My upbringing made that very clear. You might say it was a different time, when men and boys were seen as weak if they showed emotion. You'd be right. But those times are long gone. Men need to show emotion. If we don't, we'll get stuck in a vortex of icy, relational distance that will close us off from all whom we love, especially our wives and our children. We'll be left all alone with our arms outstretched, in search of something we'll never get back but could've had if we only were smart and brave enough to stand up to ourselves and say, "Enough is enough. Stand strong, soldier. Cry! Let it out! Don't bottle yourself up for decades and miss out on the very life you fought to preserve!"

A human life is finite. There's no getting back time lost on frivolous and petty squabbles, misunderstandings, and misdirected communications. Sadly, that's what happens all too often. In army parlance, it's a SNAFU—Situation Normal, All Fucked Up.

I craned my head back and stared at the ceiling for a long moment. Both of my palms lay flat down on the table. I felt as though I was lost in some sort of bizarre prayer, an alien form of meditation, or even some cerebral time travel back, back, back farther and farther into the darkness of my earliest memories, my earliest self. I recalled the teachings of Báb, Bahá'u'lláh, a holy man of nineteenth-century Persia who founded the Bahá'i faith. It now has followers all over the world. Followers such as myself believe that we should learn how to know and love God through prayer, reflection, and service to others. The faith is about giving and embarking on a quest to find peace in the tangible world through a strong belief in the essence of goodness. We believe in absolute equality between genders, and we believe in the power of education as a means by which all people can achieve greatness. It's not surprising that the educational aspect of the faith appeals to me. I believe no person can achieve his or her objectives today without a strong adherence to educational values. That was true as I came of age in the 1930s. It's still true. Enlightenment isn't just a spiritual thing; it's the whole thing. Oneness with humanity and freedom from prejudice are part of the Bahá'i belief system as well.

As I thought of my faith, the sadness that had surfaced in me as I read what I wrote began to diminish. I recalled a quote from the Bahá'i that filled me with a sense of peace I so yearned to capture and hold in my hand, like a precious butterfly adorned with the soft colors of a sunrise, the pale white twinkle of a star against the inky-black background of outer space, the deep blue of a cloudless sky closeted within the womb of Earth's precious atmosphere on a brisk autumn afternoon in the Zuni Mountains. The Proclamation of Bahá'u'lláh says, "O ye children of men! The fundamental purpose animating the Faith of God and His Religion is to safeguard the interests and promote the unity of the human race, and to foster the spirit of love and fellowship amongst men ... Whatsoever is raised on this foundation, the changes and chances of the world can never impair its strengths, nor will the revelations of countless centuries undermine its structure."

Although it was sometimes hard to see, I realized that my maternal grandparents loved Fred and me. They just didn't know how to show it. They didn't think they had to. I realized that their actions spoke louder than words, but neither Fred nor I understood that when we were just little boys. I realized that my beautiful ex-wife, Louise, had given me a great gift when we undertook the journey of faith together into Bahá'i teachings during our sometimes-happy and sometimes-unhappy marriage. A person has to believe in something more than the self for him or her to find oneness with the world we live in, and with the world of God that's greater in scope and breadth than we occupy as individuals. I think I have always known that, but for all of us, the push and pull of daily life, with its typical ups and downs, can cause us to break from core beliefs that bind us together like glue. Suddenly, we come apart at the seams, and then we fall down a seemingly endless tunnel into a fathomless abyss.

Sunrise is always the best time of day. I know I said that already. And no, I'm not having a senior moment. I'm jus' sayin', as they say in the South. The sun rises like clockwork. You can always count on the sun. It's supposed to blow up about a zillion years from now, but I can assure you I won't be here to see it. While you can count on the universe, the practically timeless rotation of the planets, and the ebb and flow of ocean tides, sometimes you can't count on people, even those you love. That was a bitter lesson for me to learn. Reality is often hard; accepting that can be even harder. But one has to accept it if peace is to reside in one's soul, one's very essence. We should all strive for the goal of peace—not conflict—as individuals, as communities, as countries. A soldier's job should become obsolete with a universal embrace of peace. Yet conflict seems to exist at the core of humanity, and even in close personal relationships. I fear that there will always be plenty of work for soldiers.

Fred and I were so young when Grandpa William took us in that we had no inkling of what life would be like after that for us. We didn't even know what a farm was. But with time, it seemed as if we weren't born in Philly but in the far, rural reaches of Northampton County in northeastern North Carolina. As children do, we adapted to our new surroundings. We settled in on Grandpa William's farm as best as we could. As little kids, we had no other choice. We got caught up in a stream of life beyond our control. We didn't guide our own destiny. No child guides his or her destiny. It's up to the parents. If the parents opt out, or die, then it's up to some other adult to take over. For the kid whose life gets taken over, that doesn't really become a great experience. You feel out of control. And you feel angry. You also feel sad.

It is often said that many black men in America, particularly those in poor urban neighborhoods full of crime and drugs, don't do right by their kids. They don't mind getting the pretty ladies and girls pregnant, and then they opt out when the babies come innocently into a world already badly stacked against them from an educational and economic point of view. The young, supposedly scary, black men end up gunned down in shootings on dark and dirty streets, or they end up in noisy and dangerous jails where their negativity is reinforced, where peace does not exist. Unfortunately, this is true in many cases, but it isn't in others just as numerous. The glacially increasing success in many segments of the African American community gives me great hope for all black people's future, however slow that progress may seem now, in 2016.

As the African American community matures over time—having risen from the violence, depravity, and terror of slavery to succeed in the 1960s as the civil rights movement took hold—peace, hope, and harmony should matter to all going forward. Progress has happened slowly since the 1965 repeal of Jim Crow in the southern states, but it has been made. As a black man of a certain wildly old age, I can see this is true. I do believe a young black man on a city street, where the police intimidate (or worse) and the gangs recruit, will find it harder to see the progress that I have seen over the last sixty-some years, in that unenviable have-not position.

Back when I grew up, black men were proud to be black. I'm not saying black men and women aren't proud now. I'm not saying that at all. Black people should be proud as hell. I'm just saying a guy who lived under Jim Crow in the South may have a bit of a different perspective than a guy who, from childhood, has been infused with the mentality of having to stay separate but supposedly equal. Sure, it was hard to deal with rampant racism, inadequate educational opportunities, and job discrimination on almost every front, but the black man back then still mostly tried to do right by his kids and the woman he allegedly loved, no matter what it took.

While my dad and mom weren't exactly the exception—child abandonment during the Great Depression was not so uncommon in white and black circles alike—they did share common threads with the African American community of today in certain ways. And as is sometimes the case now, back then, the single mom or the grandparents had to bear the child-care responsibility when the father or mother went AWOL and left the helpless kids hanging on the clothesline, flapping in the winds of an uncertain and often precarious destiny. Without benevolent or otherwise involuntary familial intervention, those same innocent kids would most often land in foster care, or in an orphanage left to rot until they got turned loose like stray dogs or cats to root around on the streets for garbage. After that, they'd head off into the misery of insecurity and loneliness that would ultimately lead to a lifelong path of nothing but despair and grief. That goes for the individual and for anyone foolish enough to love him or her.

Early on, Fred and I found out that Grandma Jennie was one tough cookie. She had to be. She ran the household, and she did so like a frightening drill sergeant. She bore one son, her eldest child, and six beautiful and precocious daughters. When we showed up on her doorstep, unwanted and unasked for, her kid count rose to a whopping eight. That's a lot of children to feed, clothe, and house. During the Great Depression, it would have been an even worse burden, and I know now that it truly was. Imagine the amount of laundry my grandma and aunts had to do each week. Hell, you get mighty dirty working on a farm with pig shit and cow dung, dirt, and hay straw. Despite the hardships, like many strong African American women then and now, she held the household together with tenacity, determination, hard work, and an abiding faith in God. She also held it together with an iron hand you never wanted to encounter when she got pissed off.

Grandma Jennie was only human. She had her own dreams and desires, many of which she sacrificed for the greater good of family and faith. She deeply resented her promiscuous daughter, my mother, Melinda, and I think she truly hated my dad, Exum. Having Melinda's two little boys added to her duty roster, instilling in her a seething anger she tried to hide but couldn't always. At times, she'd lash out at Fred and me.

"You twins are no good. You're made of the same devil," she'd hiss like a wet cat if we did something she didn't like. "You're both lazy like your no-good father. You'll never amount to anything. You mark my words! You'll never make anything of yourselves. Now, you git outta my kitchen!"

Fred and I heard things like this from an early age, and they stayed with us both for decades afterward. If you feel unwanted, you feel like you're less of a person. You may be loved, but if you don't know you're loved, it's as if you aren't loved at all. If the seed of negativity gets planted deep and fertilized with conflict, it'll take root and grow into a mighty oak within your heart. In a sense, that's what happened to me. I think it happened to Fred too. In later years, we both tried to chop down that poisonous old oak, and I do believe we both succeeded in at least trimming its massive branches. We eventually both came to realize just how loved we really had been, even though that love wasn't made apparent in touchy-feely sentimentality. Back then, as I've said, no man cried. Emotion was shown mostly in church on Sunday, when the Holy Spirit came a-callin', or at funeral services before people converged in the deceased person's home bearing platters of fried chicken, macaroni and cheese, hush puppies, and all sorts of other comfort foods.

For a short time after we arrived at the farm, we just got to be kids, playing around with the dogs, running around with the chickens, and helping out with chores that wouldn't likely get us killed. Gathering chicken eggs and picking vegetables from the garden were fairly safe for us toddlers. A barn full of large animals, like cows, can be a dangerous place for a three- or four-year-old. A horse or mule can kick your head in if you're not careful, or if you're dumb enough to rile the critter up so it hates your guts and wants to kill you dead. A little kid can act really stupid, so Grandpa William made sure Fred and I didn't get in the line of farm fire, at least in the beginning. You know, a cow can accidentally stomp on your foot and crush it. Even a bad-tempered goose (they're all permanently in a foul mood) can pose a threat, bobbing its long neck in a concerted effort to poke your eye out with its sharp orange beak. It was best to keep us little city folk out of harm's way.

But as we grew just a little bit older, Grandpa William made sure we earned our keep. After all, there was no free lunch. There isn't today, and there certainly wasn't during the Great Depression. Grandpa William had fields to tend, fences to mend, livestock to feed, cows to milk, chickens to chase, coyotes to shoot, and hay to make. He had cotton, soybean, corn, sugarcane, and peanut crops to plant in the spring and during the harvest, when the chill of October came and wood smoke rose more regularly from chimneys. When it rained, we worked in the barn shucking corn or mucking stalls.

As boys and teenagers, we woke before dawn and went to sleep shortly after dusk. The farmhouse had no electricity or running water when we were kids. When the sun went down, Grandma Jennie lit kerosene lamps that flickered dimly in the shadows, casting a yellowish light and sending soot up to the beams above to blend with the smoky residue built up after decades of cooking over a woodstove in the kitchen. It would have been almost impossible to read in such bad light, but nobody read anything, because we all lacked book learning. Grandpa William and Grandma Jennie had no education whatsoever. In their actually upscale situation, relatively speaking, they didn't particularly need it, anyway.

Ironically, Grandma Jennie would fuss and fume at us on the one hand, and on the other she'd say, "You boys study hard. You got to get an education. You got to make something of your lives!"

Education didn't much fit into our early lives, though. In fact, our schooling was sporadic, but that shouldn't surprise anyone—not really. In such an agriculturally dependent community, kids attended school between planting and harvesting, or whenever their fathers let them off work on the farm. Most farmers lacked steady hired laborers. Most black and white farmers owned and worked their own land. There were some sharecroppers, to be sure. However, the owner-operated farm was more the norm. This might go against the image many may have of the rural South in the 1930s, but it's true. Not everything everywhere is as the history books say it is. If you live history, you can tell the difference between what some writer thinks went on and what really went on.

Anyway, family was all that most farmers could rely on for steady labor. When fences needed mending, education headed to the back of the bus for Fred and me. The work seemed to never end. With 168 acres of mostly crop fields and pastures, some urgent task always required immediate attention, even if it really didn't. Together with our uncle, we twins came to be the dynamic hub of Grandpa William's prime workforce. My aunts helped out with household chores, and they did other work around the farm that wasn't considered "man's work." I've always wondered if Grandpa William ever was disappointed that he had six girls, as opposed to six boys. I suspect it would have thrilled him if the genders of his kids got flipped 180 degrees, so he had one girl and six boys, instead of the other way around.

Much of the land was flat, and it tended to flood in heavy rains, even in a fast-moving, violent summer thunderstorm that boomed loud enough to make the mule bray and the dogs bark like crazy. The water was great for the sugarcane but not so good for the other crops. No crop likes a flood. To prevent too much water from getting to our crops, Grandpa set us boys to digging canals—literally!

Later in life, when I learned about how the Panama Canal was built, I felt a great deal of empathy for the diggers, dredgers, engineers, and concrete pourers out there in the hot, mosquito-infested jungle of Central America. For me, it felt as if I'd gone to prison and was on a chain gang. I even felt a little bit like a slave. On the other hand, I also didn't know anything better, so the negative thoughts that did come came and went real quick. So we dug and dug and tried to keep smiling. We piled mud high to make long ditches that extended through the fields. We had to dig them in such a way as to carry off the water that ran in. Otherwise, the ditch would just fill up and overflow, negating the whole purpose. With a pick and a shovel, we twins, along with my uncle, made our own mini version of the Panama Canal. I have to say that when the big rains came, Fred, my uncle, and I would watch the water flow away to the creek with a distinct sense of pride and accomplishment.

Picking cotton in the searing heat was even more backbreaking than digging ditches. You had to pick each fluff with your fingers and quickly drop the fluff into a big burlap bag strapped over your shoulders. The bag got heavier the more you picked. Pick a fluff, drop it in the bag; pick another fluff, drop it in the bag. You'd do it again and again and again until you wanted to scream, "Enough! I never want to see another cotton bale again as long as I live!"

For a person with an agile mind like me, the work was pure torture, mostly because it was monotonous and mind numbing. There was no intellectual challenge. There was no great spark of genius. There was no hope of making a great scientific discovery or of climbing Mount Everest. There was just pick that cotton and tote that bale. We'd make five-hundred-pound bales of the fluffy white stuff, and it took two of us to load them onto the wagon so that Grandpa could ride into the nearby town of Rich Square and sell the cotton off for a nice profit. Textiles were real big in the Carolinas at the time. There was a constant demand for quality cotton. Grandpa William happily obliged. He'd collect the cash, and it promptly went under the proverbial mattress. Of course, Grandpa didn't keep his loot there. I never went looking for it, but I know he was no idiot. Under the mattress was the first place a thief would check. If I had to guess, he stashed the money in a Mason jar and buried it out behind the barn when nobody was around.

Fred and I had no choice but to work hard, even though I'd rather have been in school the whole time learning the things I even then knew I needed to know to make something of my life. We were kids who grew up to be teens, as all kids do, if they stay alive long enough. We grew from babies nobody particularly wanted. We were slaves to our own futures, though neither of us saw it that way at the time, and frankly, we never really talked about that period of our lives in that fashion. Only now, looking back over that bridge of time, can I see what was happening, how we behaved that way because we had to, or else. We had to earn our keep. Or else. We had to get along, just like everybody does. Or else! We had no room for negativity, bad karma, wistfulness, desire, or anything much else except to accept our reality and just get on with what needed to get done. We had to grin and bear it, and we generally did.

Still, I don't have pleasant thoughts when I drive by a cotton field in the South. It's not so much the historic connection between cotton and slaves that puts me off; it's my own experiences picking the white fluffs and toting them backbreaking bales. We'd come out of those damned fields weak from the humidity and eaten half-alive by marauding mosquitoes, the red welts rising up like itchy volcanoes. We'd go back into the fields time after time, until we had enough cotton to make those heavy bales that meant money for the Mason jar and food on the table. I have to say this, though: when Fred and I got old enough to really do a man's job, Grandpa William paid us fifty cents per week for our hard labor. I do believe he didn't pay the fair wage, because he, too, was pissed off at my daddy for saddling him with two boys he didn't really want much, except as cheap farmhands who wouldn't complain a lick if they knew what was good for them.

Working the cane fields was no picnic either. We had to do this chore before the first frost but not too early lest we ruin the crop. Sugarcane is difficult to cut; it's almost like steel. On Grandpa's farm, with no modern harvesters like they have now, we had to cut the shoots with a very sharp machete. Up to twelve shoots can grow out of these muscled-up plants. You've got to trim them close to the ground. So it was whack, slash, cut. Whack, cut, slash. Slash, whack, cut. Get the shoots down, and cut the excess leaves off. Over and over and over again, stacking the cane as we went slowly through the field. Even though we typically harvested in October, when the oppressive North Carolina humidity had greatly diminished from its August zenith, sweat would pour down our faces. The sweet smell of the cut stalks got sickening after only a short time. When you cut cane, you don't want sugar in your coffee.

After we gave the cane field a buzz cut, we hauled the cane shoots to the wagon by hand, where our cantankerous old mule was hitched up and itching for a fight. We piled the stalks up high, every muscle straining and crying out for rest even before noon. Then we drove the wagon to a long, straight processing shed. The first order of business involved crushing the cane to extract the precious juice. As the cane got squished, the juice ran into barrels. The juice was dirty, sticky, and sweet after we separated the cane fibers. We then placed the cut-up cane shoots in vats, lit a fire underneath, and boiled off the water, creating syrup that we kids loved to put on flapjacks. Sugar crystals would form with the residual syrup. The crystals were a valuable end product worth much at the Rich Square market. More cash for Grandpa William's Mason jar.

At least Grandpa had a machine to help with the peanuts. If you're not from the South, you don't know that two of the most favored things there are boiled peanuts and sweet tea. The two of them go together like a still and a bottle of moonshine. We'd set up this big, clunky machine in the middle of the peanut field and fire it up, and the thing would grab the peanut plants, suck them in the front end, do something weird inside, and presto! Zillions of peanuts would shoot out the back end into huge canvas bags. We'd sew the bags up, throw them over our shoulders, and pile them in the back of a wagon. Later, after the paved roads got put in and the Great Depression gave way to World War II, we'd pile the peanuts into the back of a truck and take them to market.

The farm had a major influence in my life. It grounded me in solid religious values and gave me a strong work ethic that served me well later in life as I carved out a successful career in the US Army and as an educator after I retired from the service. My memories of that time in my life are largely good ones, despite the emotional aspects of being abandoned by my parents and thrust into a life where my brother and I always felt like we didn't quite belong. In fact, while we were family on the farm, I never did get over the notion that we were outsiders looking in on something we would never have because of our circumstances—twins abandoned, pawned off, and ultimately reliant only on ourselves in terms of trust and love. Self-reliance would become vital for survival when we found ourselves in the bloody heat of combat in the craggy mountains of North Korea.

4   **YOUTH**

THE SNOW THEN FELL MORE steadily. I saw it whirling in the wind. A white finger of snow accumulated along the windowsill and began working its way up, as it always does when a winter storm blows in over the Zuni Mountains. At an altitude of more than eight thousand feet, my house sits so high it's like living on a different planet. The air is thinner up here. The clouds seem close enough you could reach out and touch them, perhaps even invite them in for a chat. Even

God seems more approachable up here, and in my case, the solitude I experience every day makes it easier to communicate with my maker.

I got up from the kitchen table and walked to the window for a closer look at the weather coming in. I couldn't see the horizon. The visibility had closed in so that my world grew smaller. The beauty of this spring snow took my breath away. Yes, I'd seen this sort of beauty before, seen it each day in one form or another—in the stately lope of an elk in my backyard, the timidity of a tawny fawn nosing for green shoots to eat, or the seemingly ancient spread of greenery adorning my thousand-year-old alligator junipers. I drew closer to the window, close enough so that my breath fogged the glass. Molly stirred from her place next to the wood-burning stove. She came over to see me, nudging my leg and wagging her tail. I stooped down to give her a tousle.

"Hey, Molly," I said, "would you look at the snow! It's really coming down fast now."

Molly ran to the kitchen door. She wanted to go out and play again. I don't love the smell of wet dog. I don't think anybody does. I was therefore somewhat reluctant to let her out to frolic in her snowy wonderland after she'd just dried off from her last outing. But I'm an old pushover when it comes to dogs. Something about a dog reaches into a person's heart to pull its strings of sentimentality, or maybe it's more than that. Maybe a dog puts us in touch with the primal side of our spirits that usually remains buried deep—so deep, in fact, that we don't really even know it's there. We don't remember the eons back when we lived in caves and our dogs really did serve as watchers while we slept and helped us track game when we hunted.

"You want to go out, you pesky, little creature?" I asked, standing up straight again.

Molly barked.

"Oh, go on then!" I said with a laugh.

I opened the door for Molly, and she sprinted out into the falling snow, leaving a confusing grouping of paw prints as she jumped and played. I smiled as I watched her enjoying herself. It takes so little to make a dog happy and so much to make a person equally so. For a dog, a good meal, a warm bed, and a little love are all that matters.

A dog also needs to satisfy its endless curiosity. It needs to smell everything and everybody to feel safe and sound in the world, using its nose to assure itself of its surroundings. It needs to run free and stretch its muscles to avoid feeling pent up and forgotten.

When you think of it that way, wouldn't it make sense for the same things to make a human being happy too? But though what's fine for a dog should be okay for us as well, we as humans want more than that. Based on my observations, satisfaction with just the basics doesn't punch the happy ticket for most people. We want wealth, power, status, material possessions, and property, and having some just makes us want more and more. Just as conflict seems to reside at the core of humanity, so too does an inherent underlying sense of unease and discontentment.

The Buddha says that the one constant is change and that suffering is part of the human condition that we must accept and even embrace. Happiness comes from that acceptance. Happiness is fleeting and inconstant. Happiness is not something you can buy in a store. Even though that sounds corny as hell, it's true. At least it is for me. The Buddha says that our desire to not accept what the world really holds for us as humans but to always seek more and more leads to unhappiness and suffering. To not suffer, we must accept that we will suffer. I find this concept difficult to understand. I'm not really sure what to believe, which is why I spend a lot of time giving a wide range of cerebral and emotional matters perhaps more thought than I should.

As a follower of the Bahá'i faith, I think a lot about the soul, the spirit, and the body. I think about how we as humans interact with each other, bringing joy or despair through the actions we take. I think about whether our destinies are preordained or if we really have free will. I think about why I was put on God's earth and why I'm still here at eighty-eight, soon to be eighty-nine. Most of my oldest friends have passed away. I'm the only one left of my immediate family, which isn't all that surprising, considering how old I am. What is life or death anyway? Aren't they one and the same? Can you have one without the other?

I haven't dated a woman since Louise left me in June 2012. I just haven't had the heart. Besides, I don't have a computer or the Internet, so I can't go to an online dating site to see who might be interested in hooking up with an old geezer like me. If I did have a computer and did bite the bullet and go online to find a date, and if a lady was actually crazy enough to respond, what in the hell would I say to her? I haven't been on a date since 1987, the year I met and fell in love with Louise. That's a long, long time ago. So instead, I live a life similar to that of a Buddhist monk, ensconced as I am in my solitary world in Zuni land high above the day-to-day bustle down in the valley.

I flipped on the Weather Channel on my satellite TV. I was pleased I still had reception. Sometimes, bad weather can mess up the picture, or obliterate it completely. The anchorwoman talked about April showers and spring flowers. That had nothing to do with me, especially not in a snowstorm. I waited for the local crawl to say the expected conditions. It surprised me that a winter-weather advisory was in effect for me, in the mountains.

"Interesting," I whispered.

Nearly a foot of snow was forecast to fall. No big deal, but significant for April. I padded back to the kitchen table with a fresh cup of coffee ready to go. I turned to the next page in the binder. I sat back, took a sip of coffee. I thought about getting Molly back inside before I started reading again, but I figured she'd scratch at the door if she got too cold. I built her a doghouse that evidently doesn't meet her demanding requirements. She seldom goes inside it. She is a true outside dog in that respect. She is content to roam around the yard in search of a space at the bottom of the fence large enough for her to make yet another escape attempt.

Have fun out there, I thought.

I took another sip of coffee, adjusted my glasses, and began reading again.

* * *

Although Fred and I spent much of our youth in hard labor on the farm, there were times when boys could be boys. My uncle was years older than we were. We didn't have much in common with him, and he didn't have much in common with us. As a result, we twins formed a sort of unspoken alliance as brothers. We went everywhere together. We watched each other's back, and we experienced the same things at the same time, both good and bad. If I went to school on a given day, so did Fred.

We went to a one-room schoolhouse, Antioch Elementary, that was primitive by urban standards, but for a country town like Rich Square, it was the norm. It had no running water. If you got thirsty, you used a hand pump to draw water from an artesian well. If you had to go to the bathroom, you excused yourself and went to an outhouse. Not many kids were in class every weekday. When there was time free from farm work, the ranks swelled; when the spring planting or fall harvest arrived, attendance suffered greatly. This must have upset our two teachers, Earnest and Olive Suggs, but they knew why kids were absent, so they didn't say much about it, except that we students had best learn to read, write, and do arithmetic well enough to get into and graduate from high school.

Mr. Suggs was a kindly older man who had served in World War I. As such, he'd seen much more of the world than I had. He and I spent time talking about those distant lands, and he instilled in me a great curiosity, which still persists. He'd laugh and tell jokes. He then would go serious and say, "Without an education, you'll never get off the farm, Edward. You'll work your whole life right here in Northampton County like so many of the people you know, like your friends and their parents. Like your granddaddy."

"Grandma Jennie says Fred and me—"

"Fred and I," Mr. Suggs interrupted.

"Fred and I," I said, correcting myself. "She says we was born in a big city up north. A place called Philadelphia."

"Do tell," he said.

"I ain't ever been to a city before," I said.

"I *haven't* been to a city before," Mr. Suggs corrected.

"What's a city like?"

Mr. Suggs laughed his voice warm and engaging. I always felt safe when I was with him and we had our talks. "Well, Edward, I think you should study hard, learn what you need to, and go find out for yourself. There's a big, wide world out there, outside of Northampton County, outside of North Carolina. If you want to see it, you have to apply yourself. You have to work hard. You have to want to make something of your life."

I never forgot talks like that. Mr. Suggs and his wife were like surrogate parents for many of the students from nearby farms. Mr. Suggs definitely was a father figure for me. The wonderful couple taught for years at Antioch Elementary. They'd hitch up their mule to their cart, drive ten miles or so from where they had a little house of their own, and come all the way to Rich Square just so we could get educated. They also came so they could make the small sums they got paid as teachers. They'd stay at a friend's house in Rich Square on weeknights, and then they'd hitch up their old mule to the cart again and head back home late on Friday night. Bright and early on Monday morning, they'd both be back in the schoolhouse, wondering which kids would show up and which ones couldn't because they had work to do on their parents' farms.

Although the schoolhouse was only one room, Mr. and Mrs. Suggs had a partition that separated the room into two parts. Kids of all ages had to learn together. As an educator, after I eventually left the army, I know how tough it must have been for them both. Teaching is never easy, but under those conditions at the height of the Great Depression, it must have been really difficult. Of course, they needed money as much as anyone. Teaching jobs were scarce in those parts at that time. I now know just how lucky they considered themselves. After all, they had work, and they had a little house where they lived, loved, and grew older as they tried to inspire the kids they taught to reach for the stars.

They certainly inspired me. I give Mr. Suggs a lot of credit for helping me become the man I was as a buck private in Korea and the man I still am today. I would hazard to say that every young person needs a positive role model as much as a flower needs soil, rain, and sun. Without them, the flower will die. Too much of the hot sun will burn out the life that once sprouted green and fresh from inside a hard seed. I know that Mr. Suggs had a very positive influence on my brother as well. He needed a father figure as much as I did.

Fred and I developed a network of friends our own age. Life wasn't all work and no play. Sure, there wasn't much play, but there was some. Frankly, Fred and I didn't know any better. We didn't know that lots of other kids had leisure time, though during the Depression, millions of children didn't even have a roof over their heads. On some Friday nights, five friends gathered to sing on a bridge that connected to Grandpa William's land. We sang songs together, harmonizing the tunes. We sang songs that were radio hits at the time, and the occasional church hymn. We laughed and joked and told stories. It was all very innocent, all very wholesome.

When the autumn came and the summer heat subsided, a group of us boys would grab a rifle and go hunting for opossums. We'd tramp off into the woods with only a kerosene light to guide us. We put our friend James on light duty. He had to shine the light so we could find some hapless opossum to plug. James, having something of a mischievous side, liked to put the light out at just the right time, earning the collective wrath of all the other boys. We never did go fishin' at the fishin' hole. It's hard to catch fish at night. In the daylight, we either were working for Grandpa William or we were in school. I don't regret not sitting by the fishing hole with a long stick and a piece of string attached to a bent penny nail with a worm stuck to it. Fishing has never been my thing, but I know some folks really love it.

On Sundays, Grandpa hitched up that bad-tempered old mule of his and we piled into the wagon to head for Sunday school. I studied the scriptures with the other kids. It was all very serious, but even back then, I had a sense that there was something spiritual in the world that could not be easily explained. God certainly can't be explained. The creator is too complicated for easy, pat pronouncements. I don't believe anybody can know what God thinks or wants. But I do believe each individual has a relationship with God that's completely his or hers. No one can take that away if you have faith.

My curiosity about religion and spirituality began to take root at that time. Of course, I wasn't aware of it then. You have to grow old like an alligator juniper to acquire the wisdom it takes to look back and see through the pain, disappointments, and turmoil of self-doubt to finally see the light that comes from intellectual and emotional enlightenment.

At church services, ladies sang gospel songs. Loud, boisterous, the joy in the little church was palpable. Everybody clapped their hands to the rhythm and stomped their feet as they hollered and whooped, "Amen! Praise Jesus! Praise the good Lord!" If there's one thing black people love, it's a really spirited church service. When the preacher gave his sermon, we all listened with rapt attention, hanging on every word. The man could really work the crowd, getting us up on our feet at the appropriate time for another collective, "Amen! Praise Jesus!" Sunday church was a respite for Fred and me, like those times when we sang with our three neighbor friends or went on safari to bag us a fearsome opossum.

As the Depression dragged on, life went on in a mind-numbing routine that tended to make each year blend into the next without much notice. We lived by the seasons on the farm. Spring meant it was time to get out the plow, hitch up the mule, and stand behind the animal as it slogged back and forth down a field, plowing the furrows to ready the land for planting. In fall, I knew that Fred and I would be on sugarcane duty soon enough.

But change did come, albeit slowly. In 1935, President Franklin Delano Roosevelt signed the Social Security Act into law, providing the elderly, widows and widowers, and the disabled with a safety net for the first time. During his terms, he presided over the implementation and execution of the Works Progress Administration (WPA), which oversaw massive construction projects like building the Hoover Dam. Millions of unemployed men were put to work doing any number of things. One of those things involved expanding the nation's highway system and building out the electrical grid to bring electricity to places where the power lines didn't yet reach. The WPA set its sights on many rural locales, including Rich Square.

A buzz of excitement swept through the town and surrounding farms as heavy equipment rolled in to improve and pave county roads. In springtime, the dirt roads became almost impassable, even for a mule. For a Model T, it would be even tougher. Huge ruts slashed through the grade. Mud caked the wagon wheels. It's funny. When was the last time you thought about asphalt? A paved road is just something you take for granted. Try traveling on a dirt road with a wagon and mule in the middle of mud season, and you'll never take a paved road for granted again.

Little by little, poles went up for phone and power lines. The linemen were virtual celebrities. You'd have thought they were Clark Gable. The work didn't get done overnight. It took time. But the paving and wiring of Rich Square made it feel as if the town had finally arrived in the twentieth century. Forget that it was almost forty years past the turn. Better late than never was how we thought about it at the time. When the wires reached Grandpa William's farm, Grandma Jennie bought electric lamps and relegated the kerosene lamps to use where the electric lamps couldn't go.

As with a paved road, when's the last time you thought about it when you flipped a switch and turned on the lights? Probably never, unless a bulb blew when you turned on the light. For us, having electricity meant we could read at night without ruining our eyes. I could do my homework after I finished my farm chores and the sun went down. Simple modern amenities can indeed change the quality of a person's life. That's why infrastructure is so important, both here and in developing countries. Once you build an infrastructure, you must maintain it—something our political leaders seem to have forgotten.

After we got a radio, the world opened up to us. We no longer could ignore or dismiss the larger arena of national and international politics. We learned about a place called Germany and the leader of the country, Adolf Hitler, who was making big trouble. In September 1939, the Nazis invaded Poland, causing Britain, France, Australia, and New Zealand to declare war on Germany on September 3. As I was a twelve-year-old kid in rural North Carolina, the news went in one ear and out the other. Not even the educated white merchants and town leaders had any idea of what was to come. As a country, we Americans played the role of a frightened ostrich; we buried our collective heads in the sand. News of Nazi invasions across Europe the following year didn't register much with us either. People did talk about the problems "over there," but because those problems were indeed "over there" and not "over here," we didn't worry.

That all changed when Japan bombed Pearl Harbor on December 7, 1941. Now that got everybody's attention but good! And how! It felt as if Japan whacked us on the back of the head with a Louisville Slugger when we were looking the other way. It shocked and outraged people in towns like Rich Square. The sneak attack, while horrifying, also made people angry because they considered it cowardly. The United States and Britain declared war on Japan the day after the attack. Germany declared war on the United States on December 11.

Suddenly, most able-bodied men of fighting age either registered for the draft or enlisted in one of the armed services for duty in the European or Pacific theaters. About 2.5 million black men registered for the draft soon after Pearl Harbor. More than one million African Americans served during the course of the war, mostly in the army and always in segregated, mostly noncombat roles. I was well aware of what was happening. As a fifteen-year-old in the winter of 1942, I couldn't help but be aware. If the war dragged on for three more years, my brother and I would fight too. We were gung ho about that prospect. We wanted to go fight, just like every other red-blooded American boy. We didn't understand that war is a bloody business. How could we? How can anyone who hasn't been shot at on a battlefield? It's entirely impossible for anyone who hasn't actually experienced war to imagine just how awful it really is. There's absolutely nothing romantic about it at all, despite what you see in the movies

The carnage of World War II reached every corner of our great nation, including Rich Square. Telegrams arrived at homes to say that a father, husband, son, brother, or uncle had been killed in action, was wounded, or had been designated as missing in action. It was a somber time with gas rationing and food rationing. Out in the country, we got a kick out of the idea of growing a victory garden since we had big victory gardens already, but we thought it was a good idea for the city folk to see how hard it sometimes can be to make a plant grow, especially if you don't really know how.

In 1943, when Fred and I turned sixteen, we learned how to drive the family's 1939 Chevy, which belonged to our grandparents even though they didn't know how to drive. Still, they wanted a car for practical reasons, rightly believing someone would always be around who could drive it. Fred and I would soon fill the role of chauffeur, but first, we had to figure out how to operate an automobile. That was interesting, I can tell you that! Fred and I almost certainly stripped the clutch. We both had in mind a story told to us many times about why Grandpa William refused to drive anything but a mule-drawn wagon.

He'd bought a brand-new 1926 Ford Model T. At the time, he was open-minded about driving, and he asked my mom to teach him. Now, it's hard to teach a son or daughter how to drive. It's nerve-racking at best. Imagine how it is to try to teach your mom or dad how to drive when the parent is stuck in his or her ways and obviously views the child as just that—a child, no matter how old. Mom tried her best, but Grandpa William just didn't seem to get even the basics. She became increasingly frustrated with him. As they zoomed down a country road, he lost control of the car, shot into a cornfield, and ran smack into a cow, greatly annoying the poor surprised creature.

I can still picture it. The story is one of the few about my mom that bring a smile to my face even to this day.

"Melinda, I just don't get where you put your left foot," he might have said, peering over his knobby knees at the pedals.

"Look, Daddy. See?" She pointed at his foot. "That's the clutch right there! You see it?"

"Oh! Yeah, I see it!"

"Okay, now let's try this one more time," she said. She walked him through the operating procedures yet again. When father and daughter were ready, they took off. Fast. Faster! And even faster still as my granddaddy began to lose control of the car.

"Oh my God!" Mom yelled.

"Oh, my sweet Jesus!" Grandpa shouted as the car went off the road into a cornfield. It plowed into stalks of corn, sending them flying over the hood and roof and creating a furrow. Then boom! They were suddenly out in a pasture.

"Daddy! Daddy! Look out for the cow! The cow—"

"Oh, Lord!"

Fred and I were told that the cow was fine, just slightly annoyed about getting hit by a car. Grandpa, on the other hand, came home and swore never to drive one of those dang horseless carriages ever again. He kept his word. Just because he swore off cars didn't mean that everyone else in the family had to as well, so we had a nice Chevy. After Fred and I learned to drive, we proudly drove our grandparents around. Fred and I sat up front, arguing over whom would get to drive, and our grandparents sat in the backseat as happy as a king and queen.

Our Sunday routine involved driving to church and then shopping in Rich Square. Though blacks had their side of town and the whites had theirs, we all shopped in the same stores. Most merchants knew my granddaddy, and many bought his produce, sugar, peanuts, and other goods. Most also paid him respect. They never called him a nigger, or if they ever did, I never heard about it. We couldn't order a hot dog and an ice cream soda in the pharmacy and sit at the counter to eat with the white folk, but we could buy a hot dog and an ice cream soda and take it outside.

In many towns at that time, both in the North and the South, most stores displayed signs with a hand that had its pointer finger extended. The hand's outline was painted black. Above the hand were the words "Colored that way," also in black. "That way" meant the back of the building, where there were special entrances just for us blacks. We'd go around the back, buy what we wanted, and exit the same way. The merchants happily took our money; they just didn't want us to stick around. We even had our own drinking fountains, our own place in the back of buses, and nary a white for miles around our schools and homes. Interestingly, Rich Square wasn't like that.

The only two places that openly discriminated against blacks were the pharmacy and the movie theater.

Fred and I used to love going to the movies, especially with dates. We'd pick up the girls in the car, and then we'd head into Rich Square to the Main Street theater. The downtown business district consisted of a single stoplight at a four-way intersection. It had a few stores, and that was it. The theater stood out as the biggest landmark for miles around. We'd enter the colored entrance at the back of the building. We bought hot dogs and popcorn for twenty cents, and then we'd go upstairs to the balcony, which was the designated colored section. All of this was just part of life as an African American in the rural South of the mid-1940s.

We blacks mostly kept to ourselves in our own neighborhoods. The races had little interaction between them, which is how I think both blacks and whites wanted it. You stay in your space, and I'll stay in mine. That was the mentality back then. It still is the same way today in some respects. People naturally gravitate to others who share the same race or ethnicity, religion, and socioeconomic status. The difference is today, this clustering is voluntary; back then, segregation was mandatory in the South, and not so subtly encouraged everywhere else.

As I grew older and experienced more and more racial discrimination firsthand after leaving Rich Square, I began to see that separate but equal was a hurtful farce. I began to realize more profoundly that there were two Americas, one for blacks and one for whites. I came to understand that I didn't have the same job opportunities as white men my age with identical educational backgrounds. I was treated differently than whites at every turn, and I didn't much like it. Such awareness doesn't sprout from nothing. It takes time to form and take hold. I think it took leaving the farm and going to Philadelphia with Fred to look for work for me to truly come to grips with the fact that being black in America meant I faced life as an adult with one hand tied behind my back.

5 DRAFTED

THE CITY OF BROTHERLY LOVE did not always live up to its name for Fred and me. Fred and I left the farm to branch out on our own as soon as we could manage it. We both wanted to make something of our lives, and we figured that meant heading north even before we completed our high school education. While we both knew that education was important, the impatience of youth and a hankering to liberate ourselves from arduous and monotonous farm work got the better of our good judgment. Over the years, I'd waved good-bye to my aunts as, one by one; they left the farm and migrated to big cities north of the Mason–Dixon Line to find jobs that paid a fair wage, where they believed racial discrimination would be less vociferous. A steady migration of blacks from the South to the North occurred during the 1940s after World War II.

Black soldiers who served their country bravely during World War II came home to find the racial situation unchanged. The oppressive Jim Crow laws were still vigorously enforced throughout the South. It remained very unpleasant to be black in a region where the whites made it quite clear that we weren't welcome, except perhaps as sharecroppers, cooks, dishwashers, or maids. Opportunities appeared more plentiful in cities like New York, Boston, and Chicago. Looking back on it now, I think the steady flight of my aunts away from Grandpa's farm inspired Fred and me to do the same. Mr. Suggs, my elementary school teacher and friend, also fanned my desire to go out and see what lay beyond the fertile fields and pastures of Northampton County.

When we arrived in the big city of Philadelphia, frankly, we felt overwhelmed. We'd never seen buildings so tall and streets so wide or so many cars and trucks in one place. Even the air smelled different. It always had the pungent tang of exhaust mingled with garbage. Sometimes, when the wind was just right, I could smell the faintest hints of the broad Atlantic Ocean that ebbed and flowed in and out of Delaware Bay. I'd pass by a bakery, and the sweet scent of pastries made my stomach growl. I'd pass by a diner, and the greasy aroma of hamburgers and French fries made me check how much money I had in my pocket. If Fred and I had enough to buy a hot meal, we usually did so. The clouds looked different too. I know now that a maritime climate generates clouds that are distinctly oceanic, as opposed to what you see far inland in the Great Plains. A cloud is a cloud, of course, so maybe what I observed, or thought I observed, was a figment of a young man's overactive imagination.

On our arrival, we made our way to a black neighborhood where we'd made arrangements to rent a room in the home of a very nice couple. They treated us with great kindness, and that helped us begin getting over our bad case of culture shock.

"Oh my!" the homeowner's wife said upon meeting us. "You two handsome boys are real southern gentlemen. Come in, come in, and make yourselves right at home."

We did just that. The very next day, we pounded the pavement in search of work. Jobs were scarce. It was just after World War II.

Millions of black and white veterans were unemployed and looking for work. We hadn't thought about that when we left for new lives in the big city. We didn't know we'd be competing for jobs as kids, not even twenty years old, against men who had seen combat in faraway places with names neither Fred nor I could even pronounce or identify on a map.

Eventually, we found odd jobs, but they were just as mind-numbing for me as trudging behind a plow, urging a stubborn mule to keep on moving. The bustle and constant hustle of Philadelphia intimidated me, and I think Fred felt the same way. We both felt like the proverbial fish out of water. Our hopes for happiness faded by the day and then by the week and month. The routine of working, eating, and sleeping in an urban environment was similar to our farm routine. Only the labor was different. We moved from job to job. Life seemed to consist of just working to survive. Fred and I did venture into some bars to listen to jazz and to admire the pretty female patrons, dressed up and ready to trot. But the nightlife held few attractions for either of us. We didn't drink. We didn't fit in. We were country boys, and nobody let us forget it. We also discovered that racial prejudice was alive and well in the North.

As the days, weeks, and months passed, I thought about the fact that my dad might live somewhere nearby. That idea bothered me for some reason, and I tried to force it out of my mind. But maybe the hope of running into him on the street, even though I denied I even had such a hope, played a role in my wanting to return to my birthplace. Fred and I had only seen our daddy one time since Grandma Ellen took us from the city to North Carolina just after the stock market crash in 1929. The emotional power of that meeting remains etched in my mind even now.

We were thirteen and doing some chore or another, as usual. One of my aunts came to us and said, "Boys, Mama says you got a visitor."

"Who'd want to visit us?" I asked, stopping whatever I was doing.

"This particular visitor ain't welcome here," my aunt said. "Mama run him off with a shotgun. Said he'd best not set foot on her land again or else."

"What're you talking about?" I asked. I could see Fred was confused too.

"Mama told me to tell you your daddy's waitin' on you out on the road."

"Daddy?"

"Yeah, your no-good daddy. He here and waitin' on you. Mama says not to let him on this property. He not welcome in our house. You hear me? Mama's still got the shotgun out, and your grandpa ain't around, so you best watch out for her! She on the warpath. You know how she feels about that man."

We said we understood. We hurried out to the road to see our daddy for the first time in our conscious lives. I'm sure my heart pounded with excitement as we ran to the edge of Grandpa's land and saw a tall man dressed in raggedy clothes leaning with his elbows against a split-rail fence near the paved road leading into the farm.

"Ed?" he asked, standing straight up. "Fred? That you, boys?"

"Daddy?" we asked. "That you, Daddy?"

I could see him force a smile. He did not approach us for a hug. It wasn't that kind of reunion. All of us felt very uncomfortable. Fred and I felt more confused than ever.

"What you doin' here, Daddy?" I asked."

I came to see you boys."

"Why didn't you come sooner?" Fred asked.

"Been busy. Didn't feel right. You know why."

Neither of us did know. We could only guess.

"You boys getting' on okay?"

"Uh-huh," we both said.

I imagine we said some additional small talk, but I don't recall it. Our daddy then said good-bye and good luck and walked out of our lives again, never to return. Neither Fred nor I ever saw him again. I think showing up like that was probably one of the cruelest and most selfish things he ever could have done, because it rubbed salt in wounds that had scabbed over. Once again, we were painfully reminded that our parents chose not to raise us. With help from their parents, and with hard work and tenacity, Mom and Dad could have kept us, could have raised us as their own even though times were tough. But they didn't. Mom chose to mess around with men, hopping from one to the next whenever she felt the inclination, and Daddy chose the bottle. He only showed up at Grandpa William's farm that day to satisfy his own curiosity about what his twin boys looked like and to see if we forgave him; we didn't. He had no intention whatsoever of inviting us to be part of his life.

The stint in Philadelphia was relatively short-lived. After a while, we both realized that the big city was not the paradise of opportunity we once thought it might be. Swallowing our pride, we asked Grandpa William and Grandma Jennie if we could return to the farm. They welcomed us back with open arms. When the fall came, my brother and I helped harvest the crops. We were familiar with this ritual. It even had something remotely comforting in it.

Eventually, though, Fred and I decided to try our luck in Philadelphia again. I don't know what drew us back. We could have gone anywhere up north. Perhaps we returned because we were born there. Perhaps we did because the city wasn't all that far from North Carolina, and if we had to beat a hasty retreat, we wouldn't have that far to run. This time, though, things clicked. We got our high school diplomas. We found jobs that paid enough to get by. I worked for Nabisco, and Fred worked at a brick mill. We even bought an old, beat-up car. We stayed oblivious to what was happening in the world, but geopolitical events leading to the first major armed conflict in the Cold War were already heating up and about to suck us into their vortex.

After the Allies defeated Japan in World War II, US forces occupied the southern portion of the Korean Peninsula, exerting American power up to the 38th parallel. By mutual agreement, Soviet troops occupied the peninsula north of the line. Essentially, they split Korea in half, with pro-Western support to the south and Soviet support to the north. The people of the south and the people of the North both believed they should have full power to govern the entire Korean Peninsula, pitting the West against Communist governments.

Prior to the outbreak of the Korean War in 1950, skirmishes between North and South Korea along the 38th parallel had already cost both sides upwards of ten thousand men, killed in action. In 1948, when Fred and I finally settled into our relatively happy lives in Philly, the South Koreans formed the Republic of Korea, and the North Koreans formed the Democratic People's Republic of North Korea, with the West giving lukewarm support to the dictatorship of Syngman Rhee and with the Soviets giving more dedicated support to North Korea's Kim Il-sung.

These days, when China is the only remaining major Communist power in the world, young people may find it difficult to fully comprehend just how scared the West was of Communism's influence in the late 1940s. The Soviet bear grew stronger by the day, and the bear wasn't above picking a fight at the slightest provocation. The Soviet Empire busily expanded and backed the Communist cause through numerous proxies all over the globe. The People's Republic of Korea was considered an ally simply because its leaders were Communists and they detested the West, especially the United States.

The Cold War heated up still more when the Soviet Union executed Operation First Lightning on August 29, 1949. Much to the horror of the West, the Soviets successfully detonated an atomic bomb. In 1950, the National Security Council drafted a report recommending that the United States prepare to use military force to contain Communist expansionism "regardless of the intrinsic strategic or economic value of the lands in question." The nuclear arms race had begun in earnest against a tense political backdrop, highlighted by the push and pull between the democratic West and the Communist regimes. I would play a part in that race in a fairly direct manner, but not for some years to come.

First, like nearly half a million other young American soldiers, I was deployed to fight during the Korean War. Nearly 10 percent of us got killed in action, and about one hundred thousand of us got wounded in what remains one of the bloodiest conflicts in American history. In all, the war that was just over the horizon for Fred and me ended in approximately five million people dying on both sides. Nearly half of them were civilians.

While Fred and I went about our business, in June 1950, North Korea's Kim Il-sung sent about half his standing army, 135,000 troops at the time, across the 38th parallel into South Korea. I know from experience that these guys were really tough. A great many of them had fought for China and the Soviet Union against Japan during World War II. The North Korean Army also had aircraft, heavy artillery, and tanks. The South Korean Army only had about one hundred thousand troops and a couple of planes and artillery pieces, and not a single tank! To say the South Koreans were set for a pasting would be a serious understatement. You could compare it to a grudge match between a top NFL team and a bunch of high school kids. The United States had withdrawn its last military units the previous year, believing that Korea wasn't important in its overall global strategy to contain what its leaders correctly perceived as the growing Communist threat.

The war began on June 25, 1950, and in just two days, the North Koreans pushed as far south as Seoul, the capital of the republic. Seoul is not that far from the 38th parallel, but the advance's swiftness and the South Korean retreat's quick pace appalled observers in the West. On June 30, Harry S. Truman ordered US ground forces into Korea. American soldiers went into combat five days later at Osan. The West feared that if it let North Korea take South Korea with the help of its Soviet backers, it would open the door for similar Communist conquests elsewhere.

Truman said, "If we let Korea down, the Soviet[s] will keep right on going and swallow up one [place] after another." The United Nations considered the threat so serious that it issued a plea to its member countries to send troops and equipment to help South Korea fend off its Communist enemies. Sixteen countries eventually put combat troops, naval elements, and air wings into service in Korea, but we Americans bore the bulk of the fighting. The same pattern continues today. While I know we must take a leadership role and that we have a superior military, I have long believed that our allies and any countries we defend should do more on their part. That's just my opinion, but I know for a fact many share it.

Naturally, when American troops got ordered into action, the news media took notice. Reports of the rapid North Korean advance hit the front pages of major newspapers. By August 2, the North Korean Army controlled all of Korea, except for the tiny swath on the southeast coast of the peninsula known as the Pusan Perimeter. The summer was unusually hot and dry, making fighting conditions even worse. Many American soldiers were forced to drink water directly from rice paddies fertilized with human waste; diseases were rampant.

Fighting was intense on both sides. The North Koreans lost approximately fifty thousand soldiers in their attempt to drive the UN forces into the sea at Pusan. Then, between September 15 and 19, the American-led amphibious assault at Inchon turned the tide of battle. More than 260 naval vessels participated in landing troops on beaches with tidal ranges in excess of thirty feet, meaning that any troops on the beach would get cut off from help offshore when the tide went out. General Douglas MacArthur, who personally oversaw the operation, took a big risk at Inchon, but it paid off. Seventy-five thousand UN troops landed and advanced forward with a vengeance. By early October, American troops surged northward toward the Yalu River, the border with China. Headlines proclaimed that the American-led advance would end the war by Christmas. How wrong those prognosticators were.

By then, any American not living in a cave knew that we were once again embroiled in a foreign war. Feelings toward the conflict in Korea were ambivalent at best. No long lines formed at recruitment offices, though some men did enlist, or reenlist, to fight. The American general public's point of view had a marked distaste toward the undeclared war. Congress had not opposed Truman when he deployed vast numbers of men and materiel to Korea, but war was not officially declared. It seemed wrong to some to send our boys back into battle only five years after the end of World War II.

For our part, Fred and I were like most Americans. We took note of the war but continued going about our lives. After all, if our leaders and pundits believed we'd have the North Koreans beaten by

Christmas, we had nothing to worry about in terms of being drafted. Then Fred and I got our draft notices, and our lives were suddenly no longer our own. We now belonged to Uncle Sam. We both got drafted on October 30, and nothing would ever be the same for us again, though we had no idea that was the case at the time.

We reported to the armory in North Philadelphia with our fellow draftees, got processed in, and boarded a bus bound for Fort Dix, an army base in New Jersey. The bus was crowded with fellow African American men prone to loud and boisterous talk, which continued for the trip's duration. Usually fairly quiet, Fred and I didn't say much. We carefully observed the people around us and considered many of them folks we wouldn't want to have over for Sunday dinner. When some of the city guys heard our southern accents, they poked fun at us.

"Where you from?"

"You a cornpone or somethin'?"

"No, we're not cornpones. We're from Rich Square, North Carolina," I said.

"That so?"

I nodded.

"Well, all be! They'll let anyone join this man's army."

"Suppose so," I said. "They let you in, didn't they?"

I've never been one to take sass from anybody. At twenty-three, I was tall, fit, and formidable. My wiry frame was all muscle from all that work I'd done on my grandpa's farm. I always looked people in the eye, even if they were in positions of authority. If this guy thought of pushing some issue or another, I guess he took my measure and thought better of the idea. Besides, I had Fred at my side. If he fought me, he'd have to fight Fred too.

The bus rumbled down the highway through dense pine forests until it pulled through the security gates at Fort Dix and stopped near a field in front of a bunch of buildings. Other buses were off-loading other draftees. Everyone talked and milled around in uncontrolled chaos until a giant of a drill sergeant showed up, bellowing louder than I'd ever heard a man shout. Then things calmed down real quick. He made us line up in formation, quite a feat since most of us had no idea what he was talking about.

"Fall in!" he screamed.

I wondered what he wanted me to fall into. As I looked around, I swore I'd never seen so many black men in one place before. We must have numbered in the hundreds at least. Harry S. Truman had ordered the armed services to desegregate in 1948, but I guess the CO at Fort Dix didn't care, or the army decided that black people could eventually fight alongside white people but that black draftees had to train together for some reason. I still don't know why. A white recruit can be just as stupid as a black recruit. Stupidity in the army is an equal-opportunity sort of thing, regardless of rank.

"Ten hut!" the sergeant yelled.

Fred and I looked at each other. Everyone looked around, wondering who "Ten Hut" was.

"Stand up straight, you dumb asses!" the sergeant yelled. "Stand at attention! Eyes forward! Don't look at the man next to you! He ain't your mama!"

I did as I was told. So did Fred. I got the distinct feeling that army life wasn't going to be the way the movies portrayed it. I felt uneasy, disoriented, even a little scared. This was all new to me, as, I suppose, it was all new to everyone else too.

The drill sergeant told us we'd break up into groups and draw our bedding at the supply depot. After that, we'd march to our assigned barracks, make up our bunks, and get some shut-eye. We marched over to one of the buildings and got in a line that snaked on seemingly for forever. When it was my turn, I was handed a sheet, a blanket, and a pillow.

"Next," the supply officer said, his voice monotone and obviously revealing how incredibly bored he was. "Get a move on, soldier! We don't got all night."

The noncommissioned officers marched us in line to our assigned barracks. I'd never seen such a thing. We all crowded into a long rectangular building filled with metal bunk beds with thin mattresses on top. I stowed my duffel bag under the bunk and made my bed. Whenever someone tried to make a joke, the officer barked.

"No talking! This ain't no place for joking around. You're here to train! You're here to learn how to kill the enemy!"

A short time later, the officer shut the lights out. "Now, you girls get some sleep! You're gonna need it. We muster for formation at 0500!"

The wooden door slammed. I pulled the blanket up to my chin. It was cold in the barracks. I'd seldom felt more alone, even though dozens of men in the same situation as I was in surrounded me. The next day, we lined up, or tried to line up, in formation. It was the same chaos as the night before, only this time we were bleary-eyed and famished. That began sixteen weeks of intense basic training. I can still remember marching in place and then marching for real.

"Leff, leff, leff, right, leff!"

The stomp of boots on gravel.

"Leff, leff, leff, right, leff!"

Our arms swung to the rhythm of the march.

At first, we almost always marched right into the guy in front of us, and the guy behind us would do the same. I sometimes got the feeling that we were a bunch of moving dominoes and that the right push would knock us all over one raw recruit after another. We drilled with unloaded rifles until our superiors believed we could be trusted to actually fire a rifle with live ammunition. As country boys, Fred and I knew how to handle firearms. We weren't afraid of guns; we liked guns. We both were excellent shots, which proved important when we got to Korea. But the city boys had no idea how to shoot. The first time their rifle went crack, many of the guys jumped like wet cats.

"Oh my word!"

"Golly, that was loud!"

"Soldier, you couldn't hit the broad side of a barn. You're supposed to shoot the target, not the grass!"

Fred and I smiled a lot while we did live fire exercises on the rifle range. If we weren't heading off to war, we would have found the ineptitude funny. Some of the guys we were with would never come home again. Of course, we didn't know that. We didn't know which ones were unwittingly marked for death. When you're a rifleman on the front lines, it really does pay to know how to shoot straight.

News continued coming in about Douglas MacArthur's big push north well past the 38th parallel, all the way up, up, and up toward China. The Chinese warned the Allies not to get too close to their border with North Korea. MacArthur boasted that he would take the entire Korean Peninsula, and he broadly hinted that he'd like to wage an all-out war on China. This didn't go down well with the Chinese.

Given the string of Allied victories, many of us thought we were training for nothing, getting up at 0500 and training until about 1700 five days a week. If the Communist forces were getting crushed, maybe we'd all just get to go home no worse for wear. But then the Chinese crossed the Yalu River in force in October, swinging the tide of war against the United Nations forces once again. War news turned grim as we learned about the influx of approximately three hundred thousand Chinese troops fighting against the US Eighth Army and X Corps. Thousands of American soldiers died in the battle over Chosin Reservoir. Allied forces withdrew to the port of Hungnam, where a massive evacuation by sea commenced. By Christmas Eve, 105,000 US and South Korean troops, 91,000 refugees, and 17,500 vehicles got rescued from almost certain annihilation.

We raw recruits fell into a routine, and the days ran together. We could now march in formation without bumping into each other. We knew how to fire our M1 rifles in various firing positions— prone, kneeling, and standing. We learned how to use our bayonets in hand-to-hand combat. The prospect of driving that long piece of sharpened steel into a man's chest, and then using my right foot as leverage when I pulled the blade out from between his ribs, made me recoil. I didn't want to kill anybody. I didn't really want to fight.

Fred and I were both gung ho about joining up in World War II, but we weren't teenage boys anymore. We were twenty-three and anxious to make better lives for ourselves. The so-called police action in Korea seemed far away and almost irrelevant. We knew our boys were fighting and dying over there, and we feared the unknown violence of combat. We simply didn't know what to expect. I'd lie in my bunk after lights-out and try to envision what it would be like to have someone trying his best to snuff my life out like a flickering candle. I tried to imagine the sound of heavy artillery coming my way. Then I'd drift off to sleep, bone tired from the day's physical activities, only to repeat the same process all over again the next day.

"You think we're really going?" I asked Fred one weekend when our time was our own. We'd gotten special permission to bring our car on base, and we'd drive the twenty-seven miles to Philly every weekend we could just for a change of scenery.

"It sure looks like it. Things aren't going too good over there," he said. He frowned, shook his head.

"At least we'll probably be in the same outfit," I said.

"Yeah, so we can both die at the same time."

"Don't say that!"

"Don't deny it. If we do get over there, we're gonna be in a whole dang heap of hurt. I just know it."

Fred paused for a long moment and then said, "Nobody's gonna care if we buy it over there, you know. We're on our own. Like always."

"That's not true!" I said.

"Yeah, it's true. And you know it. Mama don't give a rat's ass. Daddy don't neither. I don't even think Grandpa William or Grandma Jennie would cry all that much over us if we get our sorry asses blown off." Fred stifled a sob.

I reached over and patted him on the back. He looked at me, his deep brown eyes watery with tears. Although Fred was born just a few minutes before me, I was the dominant twin. I tended to take control of things. I liked to pretend I was in charge, even though I really wasn't.

"You stick with me, and we'll get through this scrape," I said with false bravado. "You'll see. We'll make out just fine, no matter what. You just gotta believe!"

TO WAR

THE SNOW FELL FASTER AS the morning progressed. I stood at the window looking outside, transfixed by the Zuni Mountains' beauty in the midst of a spring snowstorm blown in on the heels of a Pacific frontal system. The fire crackled and popped in the wood-burning stove. The weather may have been bad, but my kitchen was cozy and warm. I realized I felt hungry. What is it about a snowy day that stokes the appetite? Maybe it goes deeper than the conscious mind or the physical body. Maybe the clouds making shadows that change shape conjures up a spiritual connection to the universe that transcends mere petty reality. We should cherish, almost worship, the world's natural beauty. That beauty goes far in masking the ugliness that exists right alongside that which we marvel at and admire. I suppose that we'd never appreciate beauty if we didn't know ugliness as well, but I wish that weren't so. We should have no room for ugliness. We should banish it. Nothing but love, light, and joy should exist in the world.

I sighed, knowing that I was being a silly, sentimental old man. I turned away from the window and the beauty and decided to feed my body. I opened one of my cabinets and pulled out a loaf of bread and a jar of peanut butter. I took a plate from the cupboard and got out a butter knife. Methodically, I spread the peanut butter thick over the bread. Molly looked up at me with eyes full of longing. I felt half-tempted to give her a spoonful of peanut butter. She'd have to work her long, pink tongue hard to get the gooey stuff off the roof of her mouth. I gave her some once. It was funny to watch her, but then I thought on it and figured it was also just a tiny bit cruel.

"Sorry, girl," I said. "The peanut butter is just for me."

I eat pretty light these days. When you get old, you lose your taste buds, or most of them anyway. Food doesn't taste the same way it did when you experienced a favorite food for the first several thousand times as a kid. Still, I do love my oatmeal for breakfast and my peanut butter sandwiches for lunch. Both fill you up, are good for you, and won't add too much excess fat to your diet.

I sat down at the table and began to eat. I gazed at the open binder. I knew the narrative was about to get rough. I knew I was about to go back to Korea, a place I'd spent decades trying to forget. Flashbacks of combat, the horrible sights that defy all imagination, pop into my head at the least provocation, the least sort of trigger, or even all on their own without any apparent cause. I chewed my sandwich slowly, took a sip of water.

"You'll get through this," I whispered. "The war is long over. All you have to fight now are your own ghosts."

And how!

Confronting inner fears and inner demons is the only way to get well, the only way to heal a damaged soul. Every psychologist and psychiatrist will tell you that. I waited too long to confront mine. In group therapy, I admitted that I had lost much because I chose to deny the very real conflict within me, both born of the war and of my childhood. Writing the memoir was one way for me to come to terms with it all. As they say, better late than never. Too bad I waited until my late eighties, though. I wonder sometimes how much more happiness would have blessed my life if I'd been a little braver and pulled my head out of the sand much sooner.

I finished the sandwich, wiped my mouth with a folded piece of paper towel, and put the plate in the sink. Molly slept in her usual place next to the stove. All was quiet except for the wind in the eaves and the cheerful sound of the fire. I opened the stove and shoved in another chunk of wood.

"Okay, it's time," I said, my voice soft yet full of strength. I sat back down at the table and continued reading, unsure if I really could go back over the events I'd committed to paper for my own sake and for the sake of posterity. Most combat veterans keep the ghosts buried. An old soldier puts the experience of war in a box, closes the lid, and turns the key to lock away the pain forever. Some, like me, still cry when the memories come unbidden. Others, also like me, realize at the end of their lives that the stories must get told, if for no other reason than to let young people know that they shouldn't take war lightly. People die in war. Bodies get maimed, crippled, and burned in war. Minds are lost. Souls get crushed and ground to dust, leaving people empty husks that gradually fill up with hatred, despair, and bitterness that infect anyone who is foolish enough to try to come close. War is not a flashy video game with all manner of computer-generated special effects. It's real. Too terribly, terribly real.

Have courage, I thought. Be brave! You can do this! Do it for Fred! Do it for your kids! Do it for yourself!

* * *

As Fred and I celebrated New Year's Eve, Communist forces engaged Seoul for the second time since the war had begun the previous June. Allied troops fought valiantly, but the enemy's strength was too great. The capital city of South Korea fell to the Communists again on January 4 while we were back to the basic training routine at Fort Dix. The UN forces dug into positions roughly twenty-five miles south of Seoul. Lieutenant General Matthew B. Ridgway took command of the Eighth Army and ordered that those positions be held at all costs while he worked to regroup for a second counteroffensive meant to drive the North Koreans and the Chinese back above the 38th parallel and keep them there. Originally fought as a defensive war, MacArthur's push north had put the Allies on the offensive. The turnaround after the Chinese invasion in October and November put UN military leaders on the defensive again, so the territorial gains on both sides had ebbed and flowed like the tide as ground was lost and retaken.

General Ridgway adopted a new fighting tactic. In the past, American troops bypassed Communist strongholds, swooping around them and forging ahead. The tactic left large masses of enemy soldiers in the rear of the Allied vanguard, a circumstance that proved fatal to many friendly units when the battle lines broke and the enemy pushed simultaneously from the rear and the front. No matter where the fighting took place, the terrain was another enemy. Low hills, sinewy ridgelines, rugged peaks, and dense woodlands gave plenty of cover for both sides. US jets roared inland from navy ships and dropped tons of napalm bombs, incinerating thousands of enemy combatants.

Although it was nasty, we used to call the blackened enemy corpses "crispy critters" or "gooks on a stick." When the fighting got real hot, air support often made all the difference when American GI Joes found themselves in a tough spot, about to be converted to Yanks on a spit. It may strike some as odd that we black soldiers would use the word gook to describe the enemy when we ourselves were often called niggers. The paradox wasn't lost on me even then. What I know now is that in war, we dehumanize the enemy. If they're not human, killing them is no problem. If we think of them as humans with loved ones, dreams, hopes, and the ability to feel excruciating pain, it's harder to kill them. It's easier to kill a cockroach than to kill a graceful lioness. The former just doesn't seem as valuable a life form as the latter.

Dean Acheson, US Secretary of State, famously noted, "If the best minds in the world had set out to find us the worst possible location in the world to fight this damnable war, the unanimous choice would have been Korea."

As our training drew to an end, a new Allied counteroffensive that kicked off on January 16 began driving the North Koreans and Chinese back toward the 38th parallel. Losses were staggering on both sides, in part because under Ridgway's orders, advancing troops were to move more slowly and wipe out everything in their path. The days of bypassing strong enemy positions were well and truly over.

We didn't hear anything about Ridgway's new tactic. In fact, that all stayed very hush-hush. We know about it now because Korea is old news, even though that police action has never officially ended and North Korea continues to rattle its saber. Nobody but the veterans really cares about that hellhole today, and most of us are all dead anyway. Yes, Ridgway's illustrious new tactics were way above the pay grade of buck privates with only a high school diploma to their credit. By then, the newspapers reported less on the war overall. No one questioned how the fighting was going. The conflict appeared to be heading for a stalemate, and many Americans lost whatever interest they may have had in winning what had obviously become a losing battle. The families of the soldiers deployed overseas did not lose interest. For them, their loved ones' lives were on the line every day, and things often didn't turn out for the better.

Black plastic body bags streamed home by the thousands. Warm, salty tears flowed like rivers, but few Americans saw the grief of the bereft. It got hidden away. It wasn't acknowledged. It was avoided because the grief made people feel uncomfortable. It made them have to think about what their leaders did in Washington, DC, when it was more comfortable to ignore the war and bake an apple pie. In oh so many ways, Korea was like Vietnam a decade or so later. It wasn't even called a war, for heaven's sake! It sure as hell seemed like a war to Fred and me, and to the nearly half a million other Americans who fought, bled, and died in the gray, colorless mountains of a godforsaken country we had no business fighting over in the first place.

I guess it was a good thing we didn't know about the new tactics, the new military dictate that sorely discouraged the taking of enemy prisoners. Our commanders preferred that we just kill them all, and so we did just that whenever we got the chance. Of course, the enemy was only too happy to reciprocate. I feel convinced the casualty count was so high because both sides were just fine with the concept of kill or be killed, and to hell with mercy. Giving up wasn't typically the option. Prisoners were a pain in the ass to deal with, anyway. It was just easier for us to shoot the bastards and move on up the hillside.

I find it really bad that the American people weren't made aware of what we did over there and how the entire police action was built around the phony notion that Communism threatened the very existence of the Free World. The thrust of the threat may have seemed real at the time, and perhaps it was, at least to a certain extent. But the Cold War was far more of an international geopolitical construct than an engine of actual war. Looking back on it now, I find the whole Cold War scenario a little silly.

How America largely ignored its soldiers does not strike me as silly at all, both in Korea and Vietnam. Even today, it's more convenient to put the burden of fighting on a small number of servicemen and -women and their families than it is to embrace the idea that war is hell and people get chewed up, spit out, and squashed body and soul. If we did embrace that, then maybe we wouldn't be so quick to send our men and women into harm's way unless it was really necessary. It strikes me as a tragic disregard for duty, honor, and courage for a sense of patriotism we all say is important on Memorial Day but fail to acknowledge when the chips are really down. If only a small percentage of the people do all the fighting, then the majority of the people seem to get a bad case of attention deficit disorder in a New York hurry. In World War II, virtually every family was impacted; not so with Korea. That's why it's still sometimes referred to as "America's forgotten war."

I haven't forgotten.

Come the end of February, Fred and I completed our basic training at Fort Dix. We were given a ten-day leave, which we spent in Philadelphia putting our affairs in order. When our leave expired, we returned to the base, packed our duffel bags, and gathered at a train station to wait our turn to board a westbound troop train. Five hundred other black soldiers milled around talking quietly among themselves. Fred and I remained largely silent. I clutched my duffel bag tight in my bare right hand. It felt freezing in the winter air. I had my cap cocked rakishly to the right. I thought that I looked like quite the dashing soldier in my brand-new uniform. I pulled my coat closer for warmth against the cold wind. The train pulled up and stopped. Embarkation began. Slowly. Very slowly. If I've noticed one thing about the army, it's that it's almost always a hurry-up-and-wait situation. They say that war is 99 percent boredom and 1 percent terror. I think that's about the size of it.

"Well, I guess we're in for it now, Fred," I said as we jostled forward in the line into the car.

He frowned, said nothing. He'd done a lot of that lately— frowning and saying nothing, I mean. I tried to talk with him to see what was on his mind, but he said he was fine, that he had nothing in particular on his mind. I didn't think much of it either. We all felt scared. We all faced an uncertain future, or no future at all. The problem was we didn't know which. Were we the walking dead, or did we have a chance to come home again? Did God have grand plans for us? Or were we about to dance with Satan all the way down to fiery hell?

"Keep the faith," I said. "If Mr. Suggs can live through World War I, we can live through Korea."

"Yeah, but Mr. Suggs wasn't in a combat unit. We're riflemen, Ed! Riflemen! We gonna be right on the front lines where every Chinaman in the whole dang world is gonna be trying to kill us."

I nodded. "You may be right about that," I said. "Still, worrying about it right now won't change a thing. No sense in worrying about something neither of us can change. Look around, Fred!" I swept my hand in front of me. "You think any of these fellas actually signed up for this?"

"I reckon not. If they did, they is crazy as a blind woodpecker."

I laughed.

Soon it was our turn to board. Once we climbed up the steel steps and entered the car, I became immediately aware of the stink of stale cigarettes, wet clothing, and body odor. We settled into adjacent seats and prepared for the long journey across the United States to Fort Lewis, in Washington State.

The transcontinental journey was a real first for me. I'd never gone west of Philly. The sheer size of the United States amazed me. After the initial boisterous chatter, most of the men in the car withdrew into their own minds. Many stared out the windows at the passing scenery. We passed through small towns, expansive snow-covered farmlands, dense forests, high mountain passes, and mile after mile of flat, open plains. The wheels of the train made a clacking-clack-clacking-clack noise that both put me to sleep and drove me nuts. Every time we passed a road junction, the engineer felt compelled to sound the whistle. Whoo! Whooo! Whoooo! I grew to hate that whistle and the sound of the wheels clacking, clacking, always clacking. On and on we went, crossing the Great Plains. I thought about the pioneers and their wagons. I thought about cowboys and Indians. I thought about the land of the free, the home of the brave. The gravity of what was happening all became starker, more real for me during that five-day train ride west.

The snow was intense. The farther west we traveled, the higher the snow piles got. I'd never seen anything like that in the piedmont of North Carolina, where any snow that falls is mostly gone by noon, except on rare occasions. When we pulled into Great Falls, Montana, we disembarked to eat breakfast courtesy of the United States Army. The snowdrifts were at least fifteen feet high. The wind bit right through my great coat. It was fifteen degrees below zero. And all around us, we saw white faces with wide eyes as people gawked at the five hundred black men who'd descended on their community for a brief respite prior to continuing west. I'm sure they'd never seen so many of us in one spot. I think it shocked quite a few of them. Today, black soldiers are common. Back then, we were an oddity, something perversely akin to a circus sideshow. All we needed was an elephant and a dancing bear.

"Look, Ma! Look at all those Negroes dressed up like soldiers!"

By the fifth day, everyone wanted off the train. With the confined space, the close proximity to the man in the seat next to you, the bad food, we all just wanted to get to Fort Lewis. When we arrived, we settled in for still more training. This wasn't basic stuff, like how to aim, fire, and clean an M1 rifle. Our instructors gave us the rundown on what sort of combat we could expect to encounter when we went into action with whichever unit we ultimately got assigned to. Although it had all been real since my brother and I received our draft notices, the seriousness of the noncoms and our superior officers sobered us. We learned just how tough the fighting was, how terrible the hilly terrain was, and how many ways you could lose your life—bullet wounds; shrapnel; grenades; vehicle crashes; disease; dismemberment or vaporization from an exploding bomb, mortar round, or artillery shell; bayoneting; burning, strangling, stabbing, or freezing, to name some of the more obvious ones.

Soon, Fred and I got on another train, but the ride was mercifully short. The train brought us to the busy port of Tacoma. We mustered on the pier, our formation tight and our march perfectly in step. We'd come a long way from the raw recruits we'd been in early November, after we arrived at Fort Dix and began to learn the ropes of soldiering. We weren't exactly soldiers even now, but we weren't complete military idiots either. I felt a sense of pride as I looked around at the ranks of black troops standing tall and proud, ready to serve their country in whatever way was asked of them. I knew I'd stand tall too, or at least I hoped so. I wondered whether I really had the right stuff to make a good combat soldier. I thought I did.

The troop ship loomed tall above us. The thing was massive, gray, imposing. We saw sailors moving about in preparation for setting off. We heard orders shouted. It was cold out in the weather on the dock. I tried not to shiver, but I couldn't help it.

"At ease, men," our CO said. "We'll get you aboard as soon as possible."

Some men grumbled. Most of us remained stoically silent as we watched our fellow brothers in arms march up the gangplank and disappear inside the ship, as if some great gray beast had swallowed them. Black smoke drifted from the tall stack. The ocean breeze carried the smoke away. The air smelled of diesel and salt. Ships and tugs underway plowed up white water at the bow as they moved around in the harbor. For a young man like me, a country boy who'd not seen much of the world, the scene was remarkable, a choreography of a still-distant war that drew ever closer with each passing day.

Then it was my turn to board. I tramped up the gangplank, my eyes darting in every direction. We were told where to go belowdecks. The size of the ship's interior shocked me.

How can this old tub float? I wondered. This ship is going to go all the way across the ocean? Oh dear Lord!

We stowed our kits and climbed into our bunks, as instructed.

"You boys stay put!" our CO said. "Stay out of the way so the rest of your buddies can get past."

I felt like a sardine in a can. I had no space to move around. In all, close to five thousand American soldiers, plus their equipment, were crammed inside the ship. The engines were on. I could feel the vibrations. I felt dizzy and a bit sick to my stomach.

Suddenly, the vibrations increased. I heard the low, long moan of the ship's whistle. I imagined the sailors up on deck, taking in the hawsers that moored the ship to the dock. I pictured the tugboat pushing the hull away from land and moving us out toward the harbor entrance. The engine vibrations increased. I heard the dull rumble.

"We're off," I said. "We're really off!"

I lay on my back and stared up at the bottom of the bunk just inches from my nose. It already smelled in the hold. How could it not, with so many men packed so closely together in such a confined space? When the ship hit the open ocean, I felt the hull rise and fall on the first big swells rolling in from thousands of miles to the west.

My stomach heaved. I swallowed puke. I knew then that the stinking voyage was going to be a lot worse than the train ride across our great nation. It was going to be complete, unmitigated hell.

KOREA

I WAS SEASICK THE ENTIRE way from Washington State to Yokohama, Japan, where the ship docked after the fifteen-day Pacific crossing. The vast ocean amazed me. The long gray waves rolled eastward on the heels of the prevailing winds like small moving mountains. The sea air invigorated me on deck, but most of the time, we were stuck down below. Some of us played cards or craps to pass the time. Others wrote letters home. Still others clammed up and kept to their bunks. I think the waiting was the worst of it for many of us. We knew we were headed to war. We knew some of us wouldn't come back. The oppressive reality of it all bore down on us like a great weight. As I said, my stomach heaved most of the time. My fears upon first encountering the big swells were justified. The voyage was indeed sheer hell, and I couldn't wait for it to end, even though it meant that Fred and I were that much closer to combat.

When we arrived in Yokohama, the ship's motion settled down. Tugs pushed us up to the long cement pier, and the sailors made the ship fast. Army trucks with canvas tops in the rear bed pulled up to the dock, and we disembarked one unit at a time. The busy port was as frenetic as Tacoma, perhaps more so. I had the distinct feeling that I'd stepped into another world. Not in a million years did I ever think I'd see Japan, much less Korea. The words of Mr. Suggs came back to me. He spoke of what it was like to cross the Atlantic aboard a troop ship during World War I. He told Fred and I all about what it was like to see France for the first time and to hear the heavy German artillery wail in and explode with resounding concussions. He told us about the convoys of wounded transported in trucks and ambulances to field hospitals in the rear. But he also shared stories about the beautiful French girls with radiant smiles. He always remembered the food and how different it was from the fried chicken, barbecued pulled pork, and hush puppies we liked to eat on the Fourth of July.

Before I left the ship, I'd been put on kitchen patrol duty in the galley, peeling thirty thousand potatoes and cleaning pots and pans so large I could bathe in them. To say I was getting used to army life would be at least partly true. The boredom, tedium, and mind-numbing repetition of the same task over and over marked most days, or we just waited to be told what we were supposed to do next. I wasn't sure even our CO knew. He just shouted a lot. We listened and obeyed like trained seals balancing red rubber balls on our black noses.

Camp Drake in Japan was just a pit stop. Our forces pushed north again. The North Koreans and the Chinese inflicted horrific losses on us, and we did the same thing to them. It was late March. The war was less than a year old, yet both sides had each moved up and down nearly the entire length of the Korean Peninsula. Every bloody mile cost thousands of KIA and wounded. Allied troops battled enemy forces in the vicinity of Seoul and met stiff resistance. The front lines desperately needed replacements. We all knew we were about to take our bats to home plate, only we wouldn't be whacking baseballs; we'd be killing. I thought about that a lot in Japan and while crossing the Sea of Japan on our way to Korea.

What would it be like to kill another human being? The question dug into my skin like a thirsty deer tick. It sucked my blood and bloated with pregnant imagination. I pictured myself on the firing line, M1 blazing away. In my youthful mind, I thought about the Audie Murphy movies I'd seen in the theater in Rich Square. I admit I didn't think about the morality of killing for my country. I just knew in a few short weeks or sooner I probably would have to do it. I felt reluctance to a point. Mostly I felt plain old raw, visceral fear. Would I get killed instead of killing the man firing back at me? Would I be brave enough not to wet my pants and run away screaming? Would I have the courage to fight and possibly die? I know Fred thought about these things, but we didn't talk about it. None of us did. Soldiers don't talk about whether they may or may not be cowards. Cowardice under fire was about the worst thing a soldier could be accused of. It would be better to die in furious glory.

We embarked on yet another ship, and in a short time, we disembarked in Korea. I remember how cold it was. Late March in North Carolina was usually pretty nice. It could even get hot, but Korea was cold, damp, and gray. As we mustered for our assignments, we looked around like scared little kids. Everything looked strange. Jeeps zoomed around the base. Jets roared overhead. Long rows of silvery Quonset huts looked as if someone had sawed tin cans in half and lined them up nice and neat. The craggy hills rose up from the shoreline, and I knew we'd have to fight in those hills. I felt the chill of dread within me. I wanted to go home.

Fred and I were in the same platoon, a contingent of roughly forty to fifty guys under the command of a second lieutenant, a sergeant, and a corporal. Each platoon consisted of four squads with about ten to twelve men in each squad. The unit had trained together, and we would soon fight together when our final assignment was decided upon. In the meantime, we were attached to an all-black army ranger company for combat-readiness assessment and territorial training. Those guys were as tough as nails. They didn't take any guff from even the biggest and badassiest men in our unit.

"You listen to what I tell you, soldiers!" the noncom screamed as he paced back and forth in front of us while we stood in formation at attention. "You listen, and you might just live. You don't listen, you gonna die. And it ain't gonna be pretty. You hear me?"

"Yes, sir!" we answered in unison.

"What? I can't hear you!"

"Yes, sir!" we said again, only louder this time.

"You think you're tough? Do you? You think you've got what it takes to go out and kick some gook ass?"

"Yes, sir!" we all shouted in unison, even louder.

"Well, guess again, you pansy-ass little twits! You don't know squat! Get that through your pinheads right this minute! The enemy knows you're coming. He's waiting for your black butts. He can't wait to come sneak up on you in the middle of the night and slit your worthless throats right in your very own foxhole! He gonna be hiding behind every rock. Every rock and tree! And it's your job to blow his ass away! You're here for one thing, and one thing only: *to kill the enemy!*"

They told us lots of unpleasant things like that. I know now that our ranger noncoms were trying to scare some sense into us so we wouldn't make dumb mistakes the first time we came under fire. But we were scared enough when we first arrived in-country. As I said, everything looked different, smelled different, even sounded different. The noise was constant, day and night. We could never get away from it. When we went out on mock patrols with the rangers, with full combat gear and loaded packs that weighed a ton, we realized that this was no game. We intellectually knew that before, of course, but now, the war was right up in our faces. Now, we knew that our M1 was our best friend, next to the buddy in the foxhole beside us. We were taught how to dig in, how to advance up the steep hills, how to take cover when someone yelled, "Incoming!"

"Whatever you do, don't stand up!" the sergeant screamed. "You stand up, you die! You hear incoming, take cover! You hear me?"

"Yes, sir!"

They taught us how to read grid maps. We had to know how to do that because the war was fought in grids. We needed to know how to say which grid we took and which grid we lost. Our radioman had to be able to call in heavy artillery or air support if we got pinned down.

"You will be pinned down, you dumb-ass little idiots!" the sergeant shouted. "If your LT [lieutenant] tells you to scram, then you scram! If he tells you to advance, you advance! You're not being paid to think. Thinking is bad for you. It'll get you killed sure as Sunday!"

As a thinking man, I found all of this rather intimidating. How could they ask me not to think? To me, that idea seemed as stupid as asking me not to breathe, eat, or sleep. I soon learned that the sergeants in that segregated ranger company knew their stuff. I think maybe they saved my life, though I suspect luck played a big part in the equation as well.

By early April, the Allies had pushed the Communist forces out of Seoul, taking the city without a fight. The enemy withdrawal opened the door for a continued thrust north, but the resistance increased in the hills and mountain ridges in the vicinity of the 38th parallel. We were told that both sides were digging in and that every square foot of territory was bitterly contested. We were told no lies.

After our stint with the rangers, we got assigned to the Seventh Infantry Division, Seventeenth Infantry Regiment, King Company. We boarded a troop train that looked as if it had been active in World War I and hadn't received maintenance service since. The cars were jammed with men in olive-drab uniforms. I was assigned to lead the First Squad in our platoon, and Fred was assigned to lead the Fourth Squad. We both feared what might happen if our platoon got overrun; we both could die in the same action. But we didn't want to be separated. At the time, we were about as close as two brothers can get. We liked the fact that we were in the same platoon, that we could see each other, and that we were both in it together no matter the outcome. If we both got killed, we figured that nobody would really care all that much, anyway. Our grandparents would be sad, but they would have been sadder if one of their own kids bought the farm, so to speak. The danger of having us in the same small troop contingent didn't matter as much to us as it would have had we had loving parents who would miss us if we departed this dear planet in a hail of bullets or in the searing, bone-ripping heat of an exploding artillery shell.

On the train, all sorts of things ran through my head. Sometimes, I over think. It's just my way, almost to a fault. I've never been one to not think things through. I sat with my men on hard wooden benches, feeling somber and alone. I thought back on my life in North Carolina and realized I suddenly missed the farm for the first time in a long time. The farm represented pain and sadness, but it also represented a place Fred and I had called home. We felt safe there, even loved to a certain extent. We were not safe here. Not by a long shot. And we all knew it.

The train chugged onward and upward. I looked out the window and saw nothing but scorched and bombed-out mountain slopes. The trees looked like dead black hands, bent and shattered. The stands of woods that weren't destroyed looked dark and scary. I pictured enemy snipers hiding in there. Did I already have a bullet with my name on it? Anticipating combat was getting to me. I thought I might even welcome it as a change from the unknown to the known, no matter how horrific it turned out on the front lines.

When we arrived at divisional headquarters, we disembarked and formed up. The colonel commanding the regiment gave a pep talk. We started out as an all-black platoon, but plenty of white soldiers were in King Company, in the regiment, and in the division. We had been integrated at last, and it was a real sight to see. All the black and white faces turned forward, all the men's eyes focused on the colonel. We weren't the only blacks to serve in the Seventh Infantry Division. Among us were the Kagnew Battalion, a contingent of black warriors from Ethiopia. Turning to us, the colonel called us black American troopers his *buffalo soldiers*. I didn't know that the term *buffalo soldiers* referred to black cavalry units who served valiantly in the big wide West during the nineteenth century. I thought calling us *buffalo soldiers* was kind of peculiar. I could tell he meant it as a compliment; it didn't bother me that he said that.

But what did bother me was a particular white sergeant. He came up to Fred and me and gave us an order: "Get your asses moving, niggers!"

Back in the states, Fred and I had made it a point never to patronize a business that displayed the black hand, the sign with the finger pointing to the back of a building, where us black folk had to go if we wanted to buy something. We saw the boycott as a silent protest. If the merchant decided to discriminate against us just because we were black, then that merchant wasn't going to get one red cent of our hard-earned money. Of course, the merchants never knew we did this, and nor would they have cared much if they did. But we knew. That was enough. So when the sergeant called us both *niggers*, Fred and I sort of lost it. We got right up in his face.

"You call us *nigger* again, and you'll be sorry," I said. "We ain't takin' that bullshit from anybody!"

The sergeant looked absolutely shocked. I doubt any black person had ever stood up to him like that. He turned away. We thought that was the end of it, but he must have complained to the LT. We were told to report to the LT, and we got a real dressing-down. You might even say we got read the riot act.

"If there's any more of that horseshit, you'll both be separated," the LT said. "You both understand? He wasn't right to call you what he did, but you can't be insubordinate to an officer even if he's a jerk."

We said we understood, saluted, and got dismissed. I don't think the LT sent the complaint up the chain of regimental command, because we never heard anything more about the incident. We never had more trouble from that racist, bigoted sergeant either. I've always thought that the LT probably said something to the man that made him think twice about spouting racial slurs. A good many of the second lieutenants were freshly minted from West Point. They were bigoted themselves in some cases, but they were also highly aware of the value of any good soldier in a real pinch. We soon learned that racism has no place on a battlefield. The grim reaper doesn't care what color you are, what religion you follow, or whether you're rich or poor. If death is coming for you, you go when your number is truly up. There's just no two ways about that.

Our time at divisional headquarters was short. We received our divisional combat service identification badges, which we sewed onto our uniforms. The badge was a circle with a slender green border. It had a bloodred background. Two inverted black triangles, the points coming together in the center, adorned the body of the patch. The divisional insignia was similar. It featured a bayonet set at an angle with its tip pointed upward and to the right. A red triangle perched on top, and a black triangle filled the bottom portion. Fred and I were proud to serve with the Seventh Infantry Division. It was quite an illustrious unit that saw its first combat in World War I. In World War II, the Seventh Infantry Division saw pitched battle in the Pacific theater, namely in Leyte and Okinawa. Its motto, Light, Silent, and Deadly, struck us as really swell, and we loved the fact that the mascot of the Seventh Infantry Division was a black widow spider. The deadly black spider earned the Seventh Infantry Division the nickname of the *hourglass division.*

Typically, a division consists of ten to twenty thousand servicemen and women. The full wartime strength of the Seventh Infantry Division was about twenty-five thousand soldiers when Fred and I served. Within a division are several regiments of up to about two thousand strong, and those numbers get broken down to the battalion, company, and platoon level. Actual numbers vary, especially in a war zone. People constantly get killed or wounded, or go missing in action. When our platoon got assigned to the Seventh Infantry Division, we were actually latecomers. The division was one of the first to deploy after the North Koreans invaded South Korea in June 1950, reinforcing the besieged Twenty-Fifth Infantry Division and the 1st Cavalry Division as these outnumbered units struggled unsuccessfully to stop the North Korean advance south down toward Pusan.

The Seventh Infantry Division participated in the Inchon landings. It helped spearhead the American-led advance into North Korea that proceeded north to the shores of the Yalu River. In fact,

Fred and I discovered that our regiment, the Seventeenth, had actually gotten right to the edge of the river itself. When the Chinese invaded in November, the division was spread out over a long battle line and unable to resist the counteroffensive. Three battalions got surrounded and crushed, racking up some two thousand casualties in the infamous Battle of Chosin Reservoir. Our regiment withdrew quickly enough to avoid decimation. Because our regiment had suffered the fewest casualties, it led the division's drive north and was at the forefront of the combat lines. When I heard this, I couldn't help but tremble at the prospect of being in the vanguard. Some of the hardened veterans warned us that the fighting would be more vicious than we could ever imagine.

"It's bad up there. Real bad. Just keep your head down and your rifle clean. And whatever you do, don't be a hero," I was told more than once.

King Company soon found itself deployed to a forward operating base serving the Seventeenth Infantry Regiment, and then we got sent into the field. The division's overall objective was to harass the enemy and drive it off the hilltop positions just south of the 38th parallel. The Communist forces relinquished Seoul itself without much of a fight, but the North Korean and Chinese commanders stayed dead set against allowing UN forces to advance north as they had done the previous autumn. The enemy troops dug in, fortifying rocky heights and planting mines in devastated woodlands and fields. When King Company went into action, we were part of an effort to take a hill with no name. Like us, the second lieutenant in charge of our platoon had never seen combat.

Each squad of King Company deployed. All was relatively quiet as we walked toward the hill, except for the rattle of loose rocks disturbed as we tramped forward. We didn't even hear the sound of a bird. Far away, I heard the rumble of artillery like the distant presence of a lazy thunderstorm. Suddenly, the scouring sound of a fighter jet caused me to glance up. The jet flew low over the hill, circled, and gained altitude. I took some comfort in knowing that we could call in air support if we needed it. The enemy remained hidden. They waited for us to get into better range for their rifles, machine guns, and mortars. It felt creepy knowing they were watching us.

My heart raced. I was sweating. My muscles ached from the weight of the pack and all the other gear I carried. As squad leader, I took point in our small formation within the large attacking body of troops. I saw that we were out in front of the other squads, truly in the vanguard. I crouched low and began to move faster. I waved for my men to follow and turned back to climb the hill.

COMBAT

I TRIED TO KEEP FROM panting. I told myself to remain calm. But it was impossible. Adrenaline surged through me as I continued to climb the hill. It was a nondescript hunk of rock with steep cliff-like formations and natural gullies. Chewed-up-looking trees popped up and grew thinner on the higher slopes. My instincts told me to keep out of the easy ground because it created an ideal kill zone subject to enfilade. I held up my hand, halted my men. King Company was spread out on both my flanks. I couldn't see Fred, but I knew he was there, leading his squad onward.

"Come on," I said, turning to one of my buddies, "we got to keep moving. We're sittin' ducks out here."

The first enemy rifle shot pierced the air. It literally made me jump, even though I expected it. We all hit the deck as the heights above us erupted in gunfire. I didn't have to look hard to see where the enemy was. The muzzle flashes made good targets. I raised my M1 and took aim. I fired, felt the recoil of the stock against my shoulder. I fired again and again. My men did the same. The crack, crack, crack of the rifles sounded a little as if someone had lit an enormous brick of powerful firecrackers. The firings blended together into an almost-constant din. My ears rang. The smell of cordite filled the air and made my eyes burn. I realized that we would get pinned down if we didn't advance. Like a snake or a salamander, I continued forward on my stomach, firing until my clip was empty. I reloaded, jamming a fresh magazine into the gun. Mortar rounds were coming in now. The explosions were deafening. Bits of rock and shrapnel rained down on us. Sometimes, the hot metal hissed on its way past me. Our machine gunner opened up, spraying the hillside with hot lead. The North Koreans returned fire.

"Come on, men!" I screamed. "We got to get up that damned hill!" We came to a rocky area with more cover. Boulders gave us places to hide, as did naturally formed ditches. We laid down covering fire for our pals behind us. The firing from the enemy position seemed to diminish slightly, giving me hope that we might actually quickly take the objective. King Company advanced, still taking small-arms fire. The ridgeline got closer. My mind reeled. I didn't have time to feel scared. I urged our squad on. The LT screamed for us to keep moving.

And then we crested the ridge. The enemy troops retreated along the ridgeline to their next defensive position. We let them go.

Our radioman called in to regimental headquarters that the objective was taken.

"Only one KIA!" the man shouted. "Yeah, the second lieutenant bought it."

As I caught my breath, I deployed my squad to the best ground I could find and ordered the men to dig in. They immediately took out folding shovels and tried to find enough soft earth to dig a hole; it wasn't easy. I felt sad upon hearing that the LT died, caught in a hail of shrapnel after he unwisely stood up to get a better view of the battlefield and our platoon's position. The lifespan of second lieutenants in war is notoriously short. It has always been that way in modern war.

King Company had been lucky. The enemy clearly hadn't wanted to spend blood and bullets to keep that particular no-name piece of real estate. I knew that in short order, we'd run up against a North Korean or Chinese position that we could not take so easily. I was just one day into combat, and I already felt more confident in myself. It all turned out to be an illusion; even vets die. Newbies generally die quicker, until they learn the ropes of combat and understand what it takes to stay alive for one more day. If they learn the lessons of war, they get to grow old enough in combat to be called *veterans*.

The Seventh Infantry Division continued its slow push north. The early spring weather was wet, cold, and dank. On April 11, Harry S. Truman sacked General Douglas MacArthur as commander of the Asian theater. MacArthur had railed against Truman's national defense policies since the outbreak of war with Korea, and especially since China's invasion over the Yalu River. He viewed any negotiations with the Communists as nothing short of appeasement. As the spring of 1951 progressed, he called for total war on China, including the bombing of military bases in Manchuria. With the Soviets backing the North Koreans, and with the Chinese actively engaging UN forces, Truman and his advisers feared that such bellicose talk and actions could spark World War III. He transferred Ridgway to Tokyo, and he put Lieutenant General James A. Van Fleet in command of the Eighth Army.

As the days passed, our unit began to take serious casualties. We were ordered to seize one objective—a hill or a mountain—after another, and we had no choice but to sacrifice American lives to follow orders from our commanding officers. We lived in constant fear. One night, after eating our rations, we were trying to sleep in our foxholes when, all of a sudden, grenades started going off. Screams of our men pierced the darkness with each blinding flash of light. Small-arms fire everywhere. Shouts from our platoon leader. Muzzle flashes. More screams. A man near me got hit. I saw him go down just as he fired his weapon.

Night blindness from the flashes of my M1 made it harder and harder to see. We were pinned down and fighting for our lives. We poured in return fire. Our new LT screamed orders to us to move out and flank the raiders. In the end, we managed to fight them off, but we lost some good guys in the process. A certain numbness comes over you when you're in constant danger. The body can't keep up the adrenaline indefinitely. After your supply runs low, you get tired. Your feet hurt. Your brain hurts. You don't think as clearly as you should, and you make mistakes that can end up getting you or your buddies killed.

Every time we went into hot action, I worried about my brother. The fighting was intense much of the time. We were on the front lines. The enemy wanted us gone, and they were prepared to do anything to take us out. Those damnable hills seemed to have no end. We'd advance on our latest objective, moving as fast as we could along a ridgeline, when all of a sudden the world exploded into a hail of lead, mortar, and heavy artillery. The North Koreans loved to shoot up at us from patches of woods. We'd fire back at targets that were difficult to see. There's nothing like the sound of a bullet slamming into a rock a foot away from you. You sometimes see a spark. I had rounds whiz past my head close enough to feel the disturbed air for a fraction of a second.

One day, we were fighting our way up a particularly steep hill. The entire company was hotly engaged. The din of battle was now familiar to me. Screams, crying, shouting: "Oh God! I'm hit! Medic! Medic! I need a Medic over here!"

Boom! Boom! Bang! Crack!

The roar of jets flying low in formation, the muffled blast of napalm sending up geysers of raging flames ... Enemy soldiers on fire, running and flailing as their skin burned and melted away from their bones ... The whoosh of a heavy artillery shell bending its path of death through a smoke-filled sky, followed by a blast intense enough to literally shake the ground and blow open a huge crater ... The sickening splat! When a round hit flesh and bone, and the fleeting look of horror and surprise on the soldier's face before his brain, heart, and lungs stopped working ... Dying men crying like babies for their mothers.

I tried to find what cover I could, but the withering fire on that hilltop was some of the worst I'd ever encountered. I had no time to be scared. I just followed the orders shouted over the noise, kept my head down, and fired until the barrel of my rifle would have seared my skin if I had been dumb enough to touch it. I could barely see through the smoke. I could barely breathe. I felt as if my heart would explode at any moment.

"Pull back! Pull back!" the LT screamed. "Retreat!"

A good number of men had made it up to the top of the hill, but I could see the North Koreans advancing in force with heavy artillery and mortars in support. It was clear we'd get overrun in minutes. I stared in horror at the fallen soldiers from King Company. Their bodies littered the heights. Blood soaked the rock and pooled in low spots. Helmets lay upside down next to soldiers, their uniforms stained red with gore.

"Pull back now! Get a move on!" the LT screamed. "We're gonna be overrun!"

Not all the soldiers of King Company on those heights were dead. Some were alive, and I could see that they could see us bugging out. The prospect of leaving our wounded behind to get captured or, more likely, bayoneted by the North Koreans tore my guts. I fought the urge to run to the fallen wounded soldiers to give them what help I could.

"Come get me! Oh God! I'm here! You got to come get me! *Please don't leave me up here to die!*"

The fallen man's words cut deep. Tears streamed down my cheeks. I saw the enemy was close now. I took heavy fire. If I stood up to try to help the fallen man, I knew I'd die. I'd had to make tough decisions before while in combat, but the decision to leave the man behind was the toughest one I'd had to make that far. I turned away, his cries carrying above the gunfire. Those cries still haunt me sixty-five years later.

The stress of battle wears you out. A human being isn't built to fight for weeks and months on end, yet that's often what soldiers have to do. It's what we did as the spring drew closer to the summer solstice in June. Replacements streamed in. They weren't selected based on race. The KIA and casualties led to a thorough integration of squads, platoons, companies, battalions, and regiments. If a machine gunner bought it, the replacement would be a man trained as a machine gunner; it didn't matter if he was black or white. The same thing went for all other weapons specialists. We began to act distant with the replacements. Many had no training at all but were cooks, orderlies, and clerks yanked from the rear and plunked into the front lines. It didn't pay to grow too close to a replacement only to see the man vaporized or shot into bloody meat right in front of you. It didn't pay to get close to the men you'd trained with back in the states, but the bonds between us "old guys" were too strong to ignore, and when a friend died, it devastated us beyond what words can convey.

In the rare quiet moments in our foxholes, we talked of home. We talked about our favorite foods. We talked about our girlfriends, wives, mothers, and sisters. I talked with a guy I didn't know well, just shooting the breeze. We were dug in tight and not expecting any major frontal assault at the moment.

"So, you're from Philly, eh?" he asked. "What part?"

I told him. "Yeah, me and my brother, Fred, we were born in Philly."

He lifted his helmet up to wipe his dirty face. "Is that right? You don't sound like you're from Pennsylvania."

I laughed. I leaned back against the dirt and rocks and looked up at the sky. I felt nostalgic talking about Philly. I doubt I could have been farther away from there in the entire world as I sat in a foxhole in the Korean hills and mountains smack in the middle of a war zone. "That's 'cause I grew up in North Carolina. That's why I sound like I'm from the South. I guess, if you think about it, I'm from two places: Philly and North Carolina."

"Oh, well, that explains that, I suppose. I'm from Pennsylvania too. Sure do miss it right now. I hate this godforsaken place," he said.

I nodded. "Don't expect too many of us guys like it over here. You'd have to be a crazy fool to like it."

He laughed as he peeked out over the lip of the foxhole. "Yeah, you got—"

Crack!

The man's body flew violently backward. I saw a neat, round hole in his forehead right above his nose and below the rim of his steel helmet. His vacant, lifeless eyes stared up at me. Blood began to pool at the base of his skull where the exit wound blasted out a big piece of his head. I just looked at him, not breathing for a few seconds. I was in utter shock. I'd seen plenty of death and dying since we'd gone into action. As the Seventeenth Infantry Regiment kept pushing north, the fighting had gotten more intense, but talking about home with a guy one minute and having a sniper kill him a second later out of the blue was just about too much for me to handle. It was the proverbial straw that broke the camel's back.

We never did take out that sniper. He must have met his kill quota because we didn't take any additional fire. He simply vanished into the shadows of a nearby grove of trees. When our scouts confirmed that the sniper was gone and we knew it was safe, we pulled his body out of the foxhole and lined it up with the other dead. The burial detail would come along to collect him and the other fallen. Drawing burial detail duty must have been one of the most horrible jobs in the entire army. Seeing what they did, we often wondered aloud how those guys could take it. I never spoke to a soul about the sniper hit on my fellow foxhole mate from Philly, not until I began to write the story of my life. I still see the man's face in my mind's eye when he comes back to visit me in my nightmares and waking dreams whenever my post-traumatic stress disorder gets the better of me. He is a ghost from Korea who will always reside in my heart and soul, along with dozens of others of his kind: the comrades who fell and the men I was forced to kill in the line of duty to save my own life in the white-hot heat of blistering combat.

The Eighth Army reached the 38th parallel in May, stretching a battle line all the way across the Korean Peninsula. The Seventh Infantry Division, then attached to IX Corps, engaged the enemy in a major thrust of force to retake the territory surrounding the Hwachon Reservoir. The fighting went on for three days and three nights. Jets and heavy artillery pounded the North Korean positions. Both sides attacked and counterattacked, but with the air support, our troops were able to push into North Korea just north of the 38th parallel. Our advance trapped thousands of enemy soldiers behind our lines, enabling us to capture them, or wipe them out if they refused to surrender. Many preferred death to becoming a POW. I can't say I blamed them. I felt the same way.

One morning, Fred and I were on the battle line, as usual, when we were told to leave our equipment and return to divisional headquarters right away. A driver waited with a jeep right outside the regimental communications center to take us there.

"You boys are going home on a thirty-day compassionate leave," our CO said.

"What?" I asked. "Why? What's happened?"

"Your grandmother has had a serious heart attack. We just got word from the Red Cross. You've been cleared for a flight out of here this afternoon," he said. His face looked drawn, haggard, and sad. "As if there isn't enough tragedy around here. I'm sorry about your grandmother."

"Is she expected to live?" I asked.

"Sounds pretty serious, I'm afraid. She's in the hospital. She wants to see you both. She wants to see you both right away."

Fred and I looked at each other, unsure of what to think.

"Now go on!" the CO said, his voice gruff but his eyes full of intelligent compassion. "Get on outta here. You boys got a plane to catch. They're actually holding it for you! So get goin'! Safe trip back home."

REPRIEVE

A SHORT-RANGE, PROP-DRIVEN AIR TRANSPORT took us to Japan, where we caught a transpacific jet flight to the West Coast the next day. Fred and I were thrilled to get off the battle line, though we worried about our friends we had left behind. The fighting was still fierce. Now that the Eighth Army had forced its way into North Korea, it seemed the Allies were poised to repeat the previous fall's lightning advance. The North Koreans and the Chinese stayed determined to prevent that, and they ultimately did. We knew we'd been lucky, in a sense, to get compassionate leave. We desperately needed a break from the constant killing and death all around us. We worried about Grandma Jennie too. Our relationship with our grandparents had had difficulties at times, but we'd always felt grateful to them for taking us in when we had no one else in the world to help us.

The trip home was a real whirlwind. With only a month of leave total, including travel time, we had to make tracks. The army made every provision for us. Our first steps back on American soil were joyous, despite the reason why we had returned home. We were finally in the land of juicy hamburgers and crispy French fries. We craved a sweet, smooth ice cream soda. We indulged ourselves. We got some strange looks along the way as we traveled in our uniforms, our heads held high, our backs straight. The cold stares and the cold shoulders shown to us at times painfully reminded us that while we'd killed the nation's enemies overseas, the demon of racism still thrived in America. We found it particularly hurtful, and we finally understood how our black brethren felt when they returned home from the battlefields in Europe and the Pacific after World War II.

We arrived back on the farm to find everyone in a somber mood. Of course, that didn't surprise us. We learned that Grandma Jennie had indeed suffered a massive heart attack and had almost died, but the good Lord saw her through the worst of it. She wasn't going home to Jesus just yet, or at least we hoped that was the case. With God, you never know. You just don't. Like I've said before, when your number's up, it's up. We sat at her bedside on many an afternoon and held her hand. She looked old and tired. The hard years on the farm just plain wore her out. But she still had fire in her eyes. She still had a fiery soul and an outlook as hard as gray granite.

"I'm so glad you're okay, Grandma Jennie," I said. "You gave us a real big scare, you know. Fred and I wouldn't know what to do without you and Grandpa William."

"You'll have to find that out one day," she said, "but thanks be to Jesus, it don't look like that day is here just yet. Praise the Lord!" She smiled weakly and squeezed both our hands. "My, but you both look so big and tall. You seem all growed up. But you nothin' but rattlin' bones and skinny muscle. What they feedin' you over there, anyhow?"

"Rice," I said with a laugh. "Lots of rice, if we're lucky enough to get any."

"K rations," Fred said.

"K what?" Grandma Jennie asked.

"You don't wanna know," I said, beaming at her. "Stuff's horrible."

The pain and despair of our childhood did not vanish as if by magic. Yet within the context of where we'd just been and what we'd had to do to stay alive, the difficulties my brother and I had endured during the Great Depression paled in comparison. I suppose it takes context to put everything in its proper perspective, and I think both Fred and I lacked a bit of that prior to our tour of duty in Korea. As they say, some other guy always has it worse. Much worse. I realized that. I sorta knew it before Korea, but I definitely knew it when Fred and I were sent home on compassionate leave.

We ate burgers and fries while our white and black pals were stuck in foxholes with incoming heavies blasting away, the explosions so hot they'd almost burn your face off. Our guys in King Company still had someone trying to kill them every minute of every day they stayed on the front lines. It all felt very strange, disconcerting. I don't really know how to describe it even now. I suppose my brothers in arms who served in Vietnam might understand, but perhaps even they couldn't comprehend what it was like for a black guy to come home to an inhospitable land with Jim Crow still in hideous flight. Maybe all returning veterans from that war got a raw deal, regardless of their race. I think they did.

My unease, confusion, and elation at getting pulled from the blood and gore of the Battle of the Hills clouded my perspective. Nevertheless, I was wise enough even then to know I'd best count my blessings and be happy to have them. A person only has one life to live, and it's best to get at it before it's too late and you're gone for good. It took me years to truly get that straight. I missed a lot along the way. Looking down at Grandma Jennie in her sick bed, I vowed that I would make something of my life, as she always told us to. I vowed that I wouldn't let anyone or anything stop me, not even a North Korean with a rifle, bayonet, or grenade. Not even a racist pig as dumb as a lamppost or a fire hydrant—or dumber—not fit for a stray male dog to lift its leg on. Nobody, but nobody, was going to get in my way. America might have been stacked against black people, but without the good fight, no sweet victory would happen, even in its smallest forms. Sometimes, you have to start small before you build up to the big.

As time passed and our leave grew short, we made our peace with returning to Korea. As draftees, we had a five-year obligation to serve in the United States Army. When our tour of duty ended, we would have to join the army reserves. We could get called up at any time. There was no getting out of it. We hoped the entire tour would not be in the front lines of Korea. If it was, we both doubted we'd live all that long. If a cat has nine lives, then we'd used up twelve or thirteen of them already. Neither of us wanted to push our luck, but we knew we had little choice in the matter.

When you are a GI, Uncle Sam owns you. It's a little like being a slave to your country instead of to a master with a horsewhip on a steamy southern cotton plantation. The analogy may offend some people, but if you're in the military, you don't have the same rights as civilians. You don't even have the same court system. You do what they tell you or you get into deep, deep trouble. You do what the CO says when the bullets fly and zing, or else you will probably get yourself killed in a hurry. Heroes are for storybooks; they usually die young on the battlefield. Typically, no one remembers them.

Yes, we had too many close calls to count. One thing we noticed, though, was that the North Koreans and the Chinese tended to target the white soldiers more than they targeted us. We came to realize that most of the enemy soldiers were conscripted farmers. They'd never gone far from the rice paddies or small mountain farms they tended. They were mostly illiterate. They had never seen a black person before.

We black soldiers acquired a reputation for being exceptionally tenacious fighters, and we were, much like the Japanese Americans in World War II who fought with valor and courage just to make the point that they were "just Americans" like everybody else in the armed services. The Ethiopian Kagnew Battalion became famous in North Korean circles for never surrendering once in more than two hundred engagements. The battalion also never left a man behind, something I'm ashamed to say we can't boast. The North Koreans called them *superhuman* and tried to give them a wide berth whenever possible. Black soldiers got killed left and right, but if a white guy and a black guy were side by side in a foxhole, the white guy would catch a sniper's bullet first in most cases.

We wanted to stay on the farm as long as possible to be with our grandparents, visit with old friends, drive on the meandering country roads, and drink sweet tea on the porch. We yearned to go back to Philly as well, and my brother and I decided we'd do that if we lived to see the day when our own personal war was over. We applied for an additional two weeks of leave, and permission was granted. We learned that the Seventh Infantry Division had been taken off the battle line and put in reserve in June. God knows our guys deserved a rest. I guess our commanders didn't feel that we needed to rush to get back to Korea because the division was off the line, and that was fine with us. Neither Fred nor I ever wanted to see that place again.

At last, though, we had to get back, even if we didn't want to. Despite the constant racial bigotry that seemed to underlay almost every aspect of our lives during the early 1950s, home was home. We didn't want to go back to Korea to kill other men who loved, dreamed, ate, shat, and slept just like us. We didn't want to kill our fellow human beings because Uncle Sam said they deserved killing so we could preserve an American way of life that didn't serve us well as black folks. We didn't know much about the evils of Communism, and I don't think anybody really did at the time. We saw the Iron Curtain and an expansion of ideas we didn't like. We saw human rights violations, which were real indeed, yet no one said jack about how blacks were treated right in America's own littered backyard. But did we really have to sacrifice so much because we were scared of people who weren't like us? Did we really have to do that? I don't have the answers, but I've got lots of questions. I suppose I always will.

I think so much blood has been spilled because the powers that be ran scared over something they didn't understand completely. Is there evil in the world? Of course there is. Adolf Hitler stands as a superb example. Should we have feared him and his rabid dogs? Yes. But not all fear is justified. Sometimes, fear can breed irrational behavior. The Korean War was irrational. It never should have lasted as long as it did once the North Koreans went mad and drove south to conquer their brothers and sisters. Hell, if you put it like that, the damned war should never have been fought in the first place. If only the North Koreans just stayed put. If only. Looking back, neither Fred nor I gave much of a damn about the Cold War. We simply didn't want to endure more terror, grief, and sorrow on the battlefield. We didn't want to die. We felt glad to be home. Better the devil you know. Racial discrimination aside, home was where our hearts were, and always would be.

When we reported for duty at Fort Story, California, we discovered that we'd come all that way only to find out that the army had changed our assignment. We were both reassigned for duty at Camp Pickett (now Fort Pickett), Virginia. Naturally, Fred and I felt overjoyed. We would not have to return to combat with the Seventh Infantry Division. Not only that, but we'd be located fairly close to North Carolina. Before we left for Virginia, on our return trip east across the grand and expansive ol' US of A, we met a guy from the Seventh Infantry Division. We began to swap stories.

"You guys from King Company?" he asked.

We both said we were but that we'd been reassigned stateside.

"Thought you looked familiar. Seen you around over there. Wow! That's swell you're gettin outta that hellhole. When you guys leave the line?"

We told him. We said our grandma got sick and we were sent home to see her in case she died on us.

"Good Lord!" He whistled and shook his head. "Damn! You guys don't know, do you?"

"What?" I asked.

"You guys don't know how lucky you are!"

"What you talkin' about? Don't know what? What you talkin' about luck for?" Fred asked.

"I was in King Company, like I said. I 'member seein' you guys around, but we weren't in the same platoon."

"I know that. So what you getting at?" I asked, growing impatient. For some reason, I felt sick to my stomach. Instinctively, I could sense that the man was about to tell me something not good.

He lifted up his shirt. Fred and I stared at a wicked red scar still in the process of healing. It ran practically the entire length of his stomach on a horizontal axis.

"You see that?" he asked.

"What the hell happened to you?" we both asked at once.

"Gook bayonet," he said. "They stuck me but real good. Stuck me like a real fat ol' stuck pig in shit. Like as near took out my guts an' et 'em fer suppah.

"Fred and I stared at the man's stomach, our eyes wide.

"Man, that must've hurt like all get-out!" I said.

The soldier nodded, his face grim. "On the morning you boys shipped out, the North Koreans overran King Company. They came in like a bat outta hell. They were everywhere! I mean everywhere! On all sides and all at once. Almost every one of us got hit. It was a sight to see, I'll tell you. Never gonna fergit it. I sees it in my sleep. I sees it awake. I hears them boys screamin' and hollerin', and I sees the bayonets flashin' and the—" He couldn't continue. He choked back sobs.

I felt my stomach drop even more. A wave of dizziness swept over me. "It ... it was what?" I asked, but I already knew. The question was silly.

The soldier ran his right index finger across his throat, as if he had a knife and was going for an artery. "Wiped out," he said, his voice low and full of emotion. "Kaput. Dead. Almost all of us. I was one of the lucky ones, and I would've died if it weren't for the medic. I would've died if it weren't for my buddies." He sobbed and then tamped down his emotions, like most soldiers do. "All my buddies who're all dead now 'cause of them damned cursed gooks."

Fred and I stood speechless. We just looked at each other and then back at our companion from King Company.

"Sorry," he said. "Can't help it. Shit like that just gets to you, you know?"

"We know," I said.

"So your next post is back east?" he asked us, trying to get his emotions under control. "That's real nice. Real nice. Surely beats the alternative. Surely does."

We both said that we were going to Camp Pickett and we hoped he would get a plum assignment too.

"I got me a million-dollar hurt. They ain't sendin' me back. Don't know what I'm gonna do, but I know what I ain't gonna have to do no more. And that's kill gooks."

The soldier tried to laugh, but I could see that thousand-yard stare I'd seen so many times in other men who'd just come off the line. There's no mistaking it. If you've ever seen it, you know it. It seems almost as if the soul has left the body and the body is just a shell with nothing left of consequence inside. Sometimes, when I look in the mirror even today, I see that stare reflected back at me in my own deep brown eyes, my face eroded long ago from its youthful glory, my lips curved down in a grimace of grief not expunged even with the passage of nearly seven decades of living and surviving, eating, sleeping, and trying to love.

At these times, my mind suddenly swoops back to a time and place where I don't want to be, but I have no choice. I can't stop it. I have to go back, cry, and then try to move on with my life. Thank God I have a VA therapist to help me get through the hard times and stay on an even keel the rest of the time. I can only keep learning to deal with the flashbacks and the nightmares of what happened so long ago in a land so far away. Sometimes, I don't deal with it all that well. I think that has hurt me as well as the people I love and have loved. I'm sorry for that. I make no excuses for my dark days.

I don't blame my shortcomings on war. Reality is what it is. There's no changing the past, only the future. I'm grateful for the future, and I'm cognizant of the past and how it can actually shape the future in bad ways if you let it.

The wounded soldier shook his head. "You guys stepped in shit, and you don't even got the million-dollar wound! How'd you get so lucky?"

"Don't know," I said my voice barely above a whisper. "How does anyone get luck, anyway?"

"Don't know," the soldier said, patting his tummy. He winced. "Shit, thing still smarts like hell."

"Well, don't be pattin' it, then," Fred said.

The soldier raised an eyebrow, shot me a smile. "Your brother ain't no fool."

"No, he ain't," I said, and we all genuinely laughed and patted each other on the shoulder. If you're a soldier just in off the line, you're either crying, laughing, or already locked up in the prison of your mind, lost in a possibly permanent solitary confinement of your own making. You get lost in torture and pain that you think will never pass. But they do pass if you give yourself time to heal. It may take a few years or decades, but the body and mind do heal, especially if you have faith in a power that's bigger than you are—bigger than the whole human race.

I've often thought about that chance meeting in California and our chance departure from King Company on the day it got overrun and nearly every man in it was butchered. I wonder if God exists sometimes or if life is nothing more than a series of random coincidences. Or maybe everything has been written in a great big book and we have no free will at all. We're fated to lead the lives we do, and we can't do anything to change that. Yet whatever the truth may be, we just have to have faith that if we treat each other right, and we try always to do the right thing, we'll come out okay in the end. I think of the men I knew in King Company, the men I fought with, the men I protected and whose lives I saved at one time or another on the battlefield. I see their faces, their smiles. I hear their voices echo through time in the arena of my mind, that beautiful yet potentially distressing state of mind that comes over me from time to time.

Why were Fred and I spared? Why did all those men have to die? Why weren't we there to die with them? Only God knows. I certainly don't.

Later, while we were at our new post at Camp Pickett, the Seventh Infantry Division was put back on the line in October 1951. The division went on to fight in some of the bloodiest battles in the entire Korean War, including Heartbreak Ridge, Old Baldy, and Pork Chop Hill. Had we gone there, we most likely would have been KIA or MIA. So many died in those pointless battles. So many destinies remained unfulfilled because of the stupidity of misguided, bombastic generals and politicians. So many young men, black and white, died at godforsaken, craggy heights in hailstorms of lead and the hell of exploding artillery shells only to see nothing good come from it, even to this day.

Every time North Korea makes noises about its nuclear missile program, its sovereign rights, the audacity of imperial America, the devilish South Koreans, and all the rest of it, I cringe and think about the why of the whole damned disaster of a bloody war that pretended to be police action between 1950 and 1953, when the armistice was finally signed and the stalemate became odiously official. Technically, the Korean War, or police action, is still in progress. It never has really stopped. I think that's one of the saddest things I've ever had to deal with, given what my brother and I went through and what nearly half a million other Americans went through just to make the world a supposedly safer place to live.

Our duty station was laid-back in comparison to the bases in Korea. Fred and I settled into a routine that quickly became dull. The war raged on, but the newspapers didn't cover it as much. News of peace talks popped up now and again. A major bone of contention between the Communists and the Allied nations was whether prisoners of war should get forcibly repatriated. The Communists didn't like the idea of giving their POWs the option of choosing whether they wanted to return home or stay in the West. The reason why is so obvious it doesn't bear stating. The fighting continued, and so did the bitter deaths of military personnel and civilians on both sides.

*   *   *

The light in my kitchen changed as the sun made its ascent, rising in the east over the mountain peaks and traveling ever westward with the Earth's rotation. I heaved a sigh and eased back from the table, aware that the afternoon had come and was well along in its fleeting life. No morning, afternoon, or evening is ever exactly the same as the one that came before or the one that will come next. Every day is unique in a life. Every life is unique too. That's why each is precious and should never be despised or squandered.

I stood up and looked outside. The snow had piled up while I read my own story. It blew and swirled in the wind. Some spots on the deck were hardly covered. In other places, I saw that I actually had mini snowdrifts. Hands clasped behind my back, I just stared at the storm of white, and I fought the blackness that threatened to possess me as I thought about all the things that I'd seen, heard, and done in my life. I made a conscious effort to summon the joyful memories. It is possible to push away the negative. I think it's called the power of positive thinking.

Fred and I mustered out of Camp Pickett in 1952. We went off active duty and continued to serve in the army reserves. That very same year, I fell in love with and married a tall, beautiful country girl whose family were Grandpa William and Grandma Jennie's neighbors. Her name was Willa, God rest her soul. She died of thyroid cancer fourteen years after our divorce in 1971. In our youthful exuberance, Willa and I plunged straight into raising a family. I got a management job at Nabisco, where I'd worked before I got drafted, and we moved to Pittsburgh, Pennsylvania. The work didn't satisfy me. I had to do a lot of dull, routine paper pushing, and many workers at the factory didn't like having a black manager at all. They weren't afraid to let me know it at every turn.

We had many happy times. Willa and I were very much in love. We made the best of things as they came our way, and during our time together as man and wife, we brought five wonderful children into this world, three girls and two boys. Not long after our marriage ended, I decided to return to active duty. In the America of 1953, more opportunities existed for blacks within the uneasy embrace of the United States armed services than in the private sector. My brother felt the same way. We both enlisted. I was promoted to sergeant. So began another chapter in my life as an African American soldier.

10 WHITE SANDS

Darkness still shrouded the southern New Mexico desert at 0529. The air was cool, the night sky clear and spangled with fading stars. I could see the first hints of sunrise to the east, that gray-purple hue of predawn. The white, sandy soil stretched out for nearly 3,200 square miles around the epicenter of the New Mexico Joint Guided Missile Test Range. I couldn't see the craggy heights of the nearly treeless Organ Mountains in the distance, but I knew they'd soon be visible when the sun came up. Lights were on in many of the buildings. As a sergeant in the US Army in 1957, I'd recently gotten assigned to the missile range as an analyst on a team tasked with testing the PGM-11 Redstone, the first large American-made short-range, surface-to-surface ballistic missile. The entire crew of three officers, one of whom was a black captain and five enlisted men was up and anxious.

The test launch was already in countdown mode, and although we weren't allowed at the pad, we knew we'd see quite a display in less than sixty seconds, when the missile lifted off. Or at least we hoped we'd see the launch, and not a tremendous explosion at the launch site. If the rocket engine failed to function properly, the big Redstone could go up in a blast that people would see for miles. The first Redstone prototype, a design based directly on the German V-2 rocket, was launched at Cape Canaveral, Florida, in August 1953. As with much of our rocket program in those days, we relied on German scientists brought over after World War II ended. German missile wiz Wernher von Braun acted as the brain trust on the Redstone project, so designated after the Redstone Arsenal near Huntsville, Alabama, where most of the design work happened.

The third test flight in May 1954, with a new and allegedly improved rocket engine, resulted in a fiery explosion right at the pad. The engine blew one second after liftoff. Project leader Major General Holger Toftoy was not a happy camper.

"What the hell happened, Wernher?" he supposedly asked.

With a shrug, von Braun said, "I have no idea, Major General. But I will check the telemetry and find out."

"But why in holy hell did the thing go up in flames?"

Exasperated, von Braun said, "It exploded because the damn son of a bitch blew up!"

"Oh. Okay then."

The early missile program was a real hoot 'n' a holler, I can tell you that! The Redstone was still not in active army operation in 1957, but the Pentagon had high hopes that it would get deployed to West Germany the following year, and it actually was. The Redstone became the first American missile to successfully carry a live nuclear warhead to its target in Hardtack Teak, the Pacific Ocean weapons test of 1958. Analytical testing and test launching went on at Cape Canaveral and at White Sands. The missile saw active service until it was taken off the line in 1964. During that period, it earned the nicknames "Old Reliable" and the "Army's Workhorse."

Now known simply as the White Sands Missile Range, the seemingly boundless base abuts the nearby McGregor Range Complex at Fort Bliss. Together, these military installations form the largest of their kind in the entire continental United States. The area is steeped in history. On July 9, 1945, the White Sands Proving Ground, as it was then called, officially opened for business to reverse engineer German V-2 rocket technology and serve as a key location for developing a fledgling long-range missile program for the American army and air force. A week later, on July 16, scientists from Los Alamos successfully detonated the world's first plutonium bomb at the Trinity site situated at Alamogordo, New Mexico, home to a US Air Force base along the northern boundary of the White Sands range.

I glanced at my watch in the dim light outside the enormous hangar where we worked on the Redstone. I pictured the arduous process the launch team had undergone the day before to prepare the missile for yet another in a series of test flights needed to get the gyros set just right, to test the propellant, to fine-tune telemetry, to refine the deployment mechanisms integral to the dummy nuclear warhead, and to mess around with about a zillion other little things that went into creating a weapon capable of delivering a live W9 nuclear warhead weighing more than six thousand pounds down range to a maximum of 201 miles with a standard payload.

The Redstone was the army's baby. At the time, the air force was hot and heavy in developing the nation's intercontinental ballistic missile program in a spirited race against the Soviet war machine.

The emphasis was on range, payload delivery, and mutually assured destruction. The army, on the other hand, was prohibited from developing long-range nukes. Instead, it was charged with the duty of perfecting short-range tactical nuclear missiles for deployment on NATO borders to deter Soviet aggression in the European theater. You might say the Cold War was anything but cold. It was, in fact, about as hot as it gets without two sides actually shooting at each other.

The group hovered about, staying largely quiet as we counted the seconds to liftoff. Suddenly, I saw a bright light in the distance. As always, I held my breath.

Don't you dare blow up! I thought.

A fireball illuminated the horizon, and then a streak tore the sky. The Redstone was away, flying higher and higher until the guidance system kicked in and its trajectory changed to bring it on course for the dummy target. The missile wasn't carrying a conventional warhead. When it flew past the telemetry stations and achieved its preset coordinates to target, the lower thrust unit would separate and fall to the ground. The missile body would continue on in ballistic flight and then fall harmlessly to the desert below. The data collected would get handed over to us and to other teams at the base, and we'd begin the analysis process using mainframe computers about the size of a large living room.

Relieved and wired up, I joined my teammates in a subdued cheer. We had another successful launch to our credit, as did the launch crew. We had all the support needed at the range, but in the field, the supposedly mobile Redstone would be a nightmare. I pitied the poor Joes eventually part of the battalions attached to each missile. When the order went out to deploy the missile, twenty heavy support vehicles would depart in a hurry, hoping Soviet aircraft wouldn't spot them and blow the trucks to blazes. Once at the designated launch site, hundreds of soldiers would scramble into action, surveying the site, preparing the launch platform, assembling the three sections of the sixty-nine-foot-tall missile, and aligning the inertial system. The process took eight hours under optimum conditions. When the launch order was received, the battalion commander still couldn't fire right away. It took another fifteen minutes to fill the oxidizer tank with cryogenic liquid oxygen.

It may sound silly today, but that was the process back in the late 1950s. You really had to work hard to nuke your enemy. White Sands was part of the effort to make it possible to kill tens of thousands of Soviet or Chinese troops in the blink of an eye and to deliver a thermonuclear warhead across the North Pole to the Kremlin's front door in Moscow. The upside to all this scientific exploration was that Redstone technology served as the basis for launching our first satellite, and ultimately the first American astronaut, into space, but that did not happen before the Soviets goosed us with Sputnik 1.

At the time, when I first served at White Sands, we had no national news of a space race with the Soviet Union. Both sides knew that missile technology was essential to delivering nuclear warheads, but the rocket programs were all top secret, very hush-hush. Both sides were painfully aware that long-range bombers could and would get shot down before they could all deliver their deadly payloads. Our now-venerable B-52 bombers always stayed ready to fly at a moment's notice, and the air force had them in flight at all times in case of a sneak attack. As soon as the North American Aerospace Defense Command, an American and Canadian joint venture, detected an incoming formation of enemy planes, we'd scramble long-range fighters to intercept them. Our B-52s would divert to attack vectors. We desperately wanted missiles that could deliver warheads and shoot down enemy bombers before they got to New York; Washington, DC; San Francisco; Los Angeles; and other major cities in the United States.

Our missile program was involuntarily put into the spotlight when Sputnik 1 took flight on its low-Earth elliptical orbit on October 4, 1957. Boy, did that ever get everyone's attention at White Sands and elsewhere. You wouldn't believe the panic that little spitball of a satellite caused at the highest levels of the American military. I had a bird's-eye view even at my low level as a sergeant working on the Redstone guided missile's data analysis. The United States realized that it was way behind the Soviets in terms of space technology. The hustle and bustle at White Sands was made even more frenetic after the Soviets launched little Sputnik.

While the Redstone was almost battle ready in 1957, an enhanced version of it was under development for atmospheric and advanced reentry tests. The iteration of the Redstone for this purpose was called the Jupiter-C rocket. One launched our own first satellite into orbit in 1958. And while I'm waxing historic about the big, bad Redstone, few Americans outside the space program know that Redstone and Jupiter-C technology made it possible to put John Glenn into low-Earth orbit on February 20, 1962. The Mercury-Atlas 6 won a major victory in the space race with the Soviets. We Americans were the first to put an astronaut into space, even if only for several hours. I knew right from the start of my stint at White Sands that I was working on an important and historic rocket, a rocket that literally changed the world. When I was part of the analysis team at White Sands, I was a very proud man, especially given what it took me to get the job as an African American with no college education.

Willa and I didn't wind up in New Mexico right away. After I enlisted, I served with a military police unit in Maryland. The duty didn't suit me much. Our main mission involved tracking down soldiers who were absent without leave. A guy who has gone AWOL will not want to come peacefully back to face disciplinary action, a dishonorable discharge, or even the stockade, depending on the circumstances. He's going to resist, run, or fight. At the very least, he will be in an extremely bad mood. As a black man with an MP band in prominent display on my arm, I was subjected to a level of resentment I'd seldom encountered before in the army. I recall arresting a white soldier after we caught him for going AWOL. I took out the handcuffs, per procedure.

"You can't do this!" the man hissed.

"I'm sorry, soldier, but the regs say I got to cuff you before I take you in."

"You dirty damned nigger! You got no right!"

"Sassin' me like that ain't going to do you one bit of good, soldier," I said as I pulled his hands roughly behind his back and cuffed him. I'd long since gotten over feeling hurt or inferior when someone called me nigger, but I never stopped getting angry about it.

I quickly put in for a transfer. My CO was good about processing it, and I found myself going back to Korea for a new tour with the Seventh Infantry Division. The war was over, and the Seventh Infantry Division was still stationed in Japan. I regretted having to leave Willa all alone until I could send for her, but such was army life. You go where you're sent, and besides, I'd asked for a transfer. In a way, I felt as if I was going home. The men of the Seventh Infantry Division were fabulous soldiers, and I proudly served with them.

Unless you've been in logistical support in the armed services, you have no idea how much stuff it takes to run an army in the field. With the war over, there was no need to have thousands and thousands of half-tons, jeeps, armored personnel carriers, halftracks, and other army vehicles in Korea. The high command wanted any surplus vehicles removed from Korea and placed in central depots that would serve the Asian theater. I got assigned to a massive one in Japan, the Tokozorow Ordnance Depot. I was essentially a glorified clerk, a noncom in charge of more than eight hundred Japanese employed by the army. The culture was alien to me, as was the language.

I soon noticed that the guys would laugh when I came around. I had no idea what they talked about. I had to rely on the translator to break the language barrier. It didn't take me long to figure out that they probably said some pretty nasty things about me right to my face, so I took action. I got hold of a couple of college-educated Japanese guys who spoke some English, sat them down, and presented what I thought sounded like a reasonable proposal.

"You want to improve your English?" I asked.

The two guys nodded enthusiastically.

"Well, I want to learn how to speak Japanese. If you teach me, I'll teach you. We can all learn together."

Again, they nodded enthusiastically.

And that's how I learned Japanese. I became so fluent in the language that people thought I could have been born in Japan. Clerking at the depot got easier. The Japanese employees respected the fact that I'd taken the time and effort to learn how to speak with them in their native tongue. I saw it as a way to cover my six, but I also felt a great deal of satisfaction about being bilingual. I brought Willa and the two kids over, and I served at the depot for about two years. Those were happy years. The family fit in with others at the base, and because I could speak Japanese, I was accepted more readily when we went off base grounds.

Still, as had been the case earlier in my life, I grew discontented. I couldn't see that the job I did for the army opened up anything good for me in civilian life. I was not on a stellar career path in the army. I had no formal schooling outside of high school. That meant I'd never become an officer. You need a four-year college degree to step into the officer camp, and I didn't have one, nor did it look as if I'd get one anytime soon. Officer training school didn't look even remotely possible.

One day, I'd had enough of tracking the thousands of vehicles in my charge. It was my responsibility to assist the officers running the depot. When an order for a jeep came through, we'd ship it off to the base that requested it. We also rehabbed old vehicles, cannibalized others for parts, and even rebuilt a fleet of Chevy sedans for use by the officers. It looked as if we had half the army vehicles in the whole damn world right there at Tokozorow. If they all tried to go at once, we'd have had a traffic jam all the way to Tokyo.

I'd heard that a duty at White Sands could act as a springboard to better things. In particular, there was apparently an opening on the top-secret Redstone project. I had no idea what a Redstone was, but it sounded intriguing. Everybody knew White Sands and missiles went together, so I figured Redstone must be some sort of missile. I strode purposefully into my CO's office with a grand plan in mind to make something of my life, not just rot away in the backwaters of the army until I could retire with a pension and veteran medical benefits.

"I want to apply for the slot on the Redstone project," I said, after explaining that I was hoping for more challenging duties.

My CO smiled. "Sergeant Smith, you think you got what it takes to work on guided missiles?"

"Yes, sir," I said. "All I need is a chance."

"Uh-huh. Sure you do. You do realize that you'll have to get top-secret clearance before you can get within spitting distance of the front gate."

"I wasn't aware."

"Well, it's true. There are a lot of guys applying for the slot. I'm told that the program is ramping up. They're pulling in civilian scientists who know a thing or two about gyros, telemetry, all that sort of crap. The civvies and the army technical personnel need support staff. That's where you'd come in, if you're chosen."

I raised an eyebrow. "So, is it okay to apply, sir? Would you approve my transfer if I get in?"

He nodded. "Hate to lose you, though. Seems you know the whereabouts of every single damned vehicle we got around here."

"I do," I said, and then regretted it. I didn't want to give the CO an excuse to keep me at Tokozorow.

"Dismissed, Sergeant," he said. I saluted and turned to go. "Sergeant?" the CO said.

I turned around again. "Yes, sir?"

"Good luck! I know you're a smart guy. A bit pushy sometimes, but a smart guy. You might like the work you do at White Sands. Guess there's only one way you're going to find out, and that's to get your clearance and start working on the Redstone."

"Thank you, sir," I said.

"Well, don't thank me. Thank President Truman for signing that executive order back in 1948. Dismissed."

"Yes, sir!" I said, giving him a crisp salute. I wheeled around and marched out of his office with pride bubbling up inside me. When I told Willa about my plan, she supported it. I think she felt ready to head back stateside. The army gave me a bunch of tests to see whether I had the potential to work on a highly technical project like the Redstone. One was an IQ test. The test administrator barely contained his surprise when he told me I'd scored 146.

"That's one point over genius, Sergeant," he said.

"That's good, I suppose," I said.

"I'll say," he said. "Congratulations. That score will help you get where you want to be in this man's army."

"Hope so," I said. "I'm tired of pushing paper around."

I wasn't book smart yet. That would come later, after I went to a four-year college and got a bachelor of arts degree in business administration. However, I was life smart. Fred and I had to be. Otherwise, we wouldn't have survived as we had without turning into angry, bitter young black men. At all times, we tried to make the best of what we received, and when we weren't satisfied and thought we could do better, we never were afraid to try. And try hard. By this time, Fred served in an army unit in France. He'd also married a lovely woman.

A short time after requesting the transfer, the army flew me stateside to Travis Air Force Base in Fairfield, California. The investigators put me through more tests, questioned me about everything under the sun, and went through a strict background check on my life. The exercise was meant to see if I qualified for work on the Redstone project and for the top-secret clearance I'd need to do my job as a guided missile analyst.

"Why do you want to work on the Redstone project?" they'd ask over and over.

"I want to learn about new technology. I want to know about rocket ships!" I said.

"That so. Why? What would a man like you want to know about outer space? Why do you even care about rocket ships?"

"Because they go into outer space!"

"Not yet, they don't, or at least not for very long."

"They will! And I want to help make that happen!"

"How do you feel about Commies?"

I actually didn't like them much. Communists killed a bunch of my buddies in Korea. I had no trouble saying that I didn't want any over for Sunday dinner.

"Have you ever been a Commie?" the stern, white senior investigator asked.

"Sir, I didn't even know what a Communist was until I got drafted. Then I found out real quick."

"Anyone you know a Commie?"

"Nope," I said.

"So you're interested in space." The investigator seemed to be changing the subject back to something I was more interested in.

"Yes, sir!"

"The Redstone isn't necessarily about space. It's about developing a weapon for the army in case the Commies invade West Germany. You got a problem with that?"

"No, sir!"

"It's not about space at all."

"We'll let you know," the investigator said. With that, the meeting concluded.

I didn't know it at the time, but well more than three hundred soldiers had applied for the single open analyst job. I nursed an intense hope, a dream almost, of getting sent to White Sands. I got good recommendations from my white CO. I had a combat record with two offensive operation stars, a presidential citation medal for service in Korea, and others. I had a high IQ. And best of all, I came from the ordnance department. I knew how to process lots of data to keep everything running smoothly in a very complicated and busy depot. When I found out I'd been accepted, I brimmed with pride.

A short time later, I found myself reporting for duty at White Sands. I was told that I had to find quarters for my family off the base grounds. It took me almost a month to find a place where the landlord would rent to a black family. I admit I was getting tired of the segregation, the unequal treatment outside the military. But as a black man, I had no legal right to complain or press any kind of charges. Today, the situation seems unthinkable, but it was reality in the late 1950s.

As I drove around, the land's flatness surprised me. I saw nothing but whitish sand, tawny rocks, a few bits of green in places. Rugged purple-gray mountains protruded from the flatness like rotten teeth. If ever there was a place of desolation, the desert of southern New Mexico was it. I suppose that's why the military chose it as the location to test missiles, artillery, and a nuclear bomb. It took awhile, but I finally found an all-black neighborhood with pretty nice homes.

When I reported for duty, I noticed black civilians and black soldiers on base. There were also a lot of white guys from Alabama,

Mississippi, and Louisiana. They made it no secret that they didn't like us. We didn't like them either. We interacted politely for the most part. My white CO was first-rate, but I soon realized that I was in a tough spot, not knowing anything about computers.

"It's sink or swim, Sergeant Smith," one of my COs said early on. "You get with the program, or you're out."

Computers in those days used punch-card input and output for data management. The machines were big, cumbersome, and expensive. Data techs would process our test results, and we'd analyze them to fine-tune various missile components. I received instructions from teammates who knew the ropes, and I caught on fast enough to not get bounced from the program. As the arms and space race heated up in 1950 and 1958, we were among the thousands of people involved in making sure America came out on top. Those days opened my eyes to the future. They let me see how important it was to harness the power of technology, though I hoped to harness it for practical purposes, not to wage war.

When my tour at White Sands was up, my CO called me into his office and said, if I reenlisted, my next duty station would be in Germany. I thanked him, went home, discussed the matter with Willa, and decided not to re-up. Moving the family all the way to Germany just didn't sit right. I saw that advancement in the army still remained relatively closed to soldiers without a formal college education.

I kept hearing Grandma Jennie's voice in my head. "Ed, you got to work hard. You got to make something of your life!"

My wife and kids and I said good-bye to our friends in the all-black neighborhood where we'd spent so many happy hours. We pulled away and turned the car east, back to North Carolina, where we'd both grown up.

* * *

The telephone rang, actually startling me. I stopped reading, noting that I was pretty much done with the story. So much had happened between late 1959 and the present, but that period subsequent to my thirty-second year after leaving active duty and joining the National Guard represented a different sort of story. I'd formed as a man, as a husband, as a father. I felt secure in my own skin, and I had big plans for the future that I thought might come to fruition and manifest in a better life for my family.

I got up to pick up the phone, looking out the window as I did. Molly followed me and nudged my leg, her little tail wagging. It was still snowing, only not as hard as before.

"Hello?"

"Dad? Everything okay? Been snowing like anything all day."

"Hi, Gil!" I said, always pleased to hear from my son. "Yeah, everything's fine. Snow looks so pretty in the junipers. It's like they got a new coat on."

Gil laughed. "You want me to come over and plow the driveway?"

I thought about that for a moment. By the time Gil drove the thirty miles out to Zuni Canyon Road, it would be getting late. He'd have to hitch the plow blade to the riding mower and then run the mower-turned-plow down the drive. The driveway is a flat grade, but I still didn't think he needed to go to the trouble.

"I think I'll be fine. Snow'll melt by tomorrow, anyway."

"Not if it doesn't get warmer."

"Suppose so," I said. There was a long moment of silence. "I'm just about done reading my story," I said. I suddenly felt tired, like every bit of my eighty-eight, soon-to-be eighty-nine, years.

"You don't say," Gil said. "How'd it go? You happy with it?"

All six of my kids, two sons and three daughters by Willa and a son by Louise, had encouraged me to write down my thoughts and experiences. They said it would do me good. My therapist agreed. I felt warm at heart when I thought of my kids. Their support and love have long sustained me through sometimes-lonely times, and have long made me feel as if something of me would be left behind when the good Lord finally decides to call me home.

If you have been loved, then you have lived. If you are remembered fondly after you pass away, you haven't really died and left the world. You are still part of it, entwined in its very fabric, in the long continuum that is humanity itself. We are but small particles of dust in the context of those who came before us and those who will follow. The rising sun, the ocean, the wind, the stars—none of these things knows or cares about who we are, who we once were, and what we might become in the future. When we die, the natural world continues as if we never existed. Only in others' memories can a person find even a hint of immortality, some semblance of peace in knowing that at least we mattered to someone.

"It was hard to read at times, like in Korea," I said. I stooped and gave Molly a ruffle on her furry head. The little mutt licked my hand. I grinned as I stood up again, feeling the residue of the painful memories begin to fade.

"Yeah, Dad, I can only imagine. You never did talk much about what happened over there. I'm gonna learn a thing or two about you, maybe?"

"I'd say that's a possibility."

"Look forward to reading your story," he said. He let out a sigh. "So, you sure you don't want me to drive out there? It's no big deal. Roads aren't too bad."

"You stay put, son," I said. "I got Molly to keep me company."

"I'll be out tomorrow then, okay?"

I told Gil that would be great, that I'd have a pot of coffee waiting for him. Then we said good-bye.

The sun started to sink low behind the Zuni Mountains. The snow tapered off. It had been a strange day, special in its own way, a kind of quiet milestone in an old man's long life. Sometimes, it's important to look back to where you've been to see how you're doing in the present. I thought, all things considered, I'd done just fine.

I squatted down and called to Molly. "Come on, Molly! Bet you want to go out! You wanna go out to play in the snow?"

The dog barked and jumped up and down, as if to say, "Yippee! Let's go!"

I opened the door, and Molly zoomed outside, leaving fresh paw prints in the newly fallen snow.

"I think I might just join you," I said, and went back inside to get my warm coat.

EPILOGUE

WHEN I LEFT ACTIVE ARMY duty, I felt determined to make something more of my life. I understood that education offered me the most likely way out of a life of dead-end jobs. I'd always loved learning. My time and challenges at White Sands inspired me and filled me with the self-confidence I needed.

I applied to and was accepted at North Carolina Agricultural and Technical State University in Greensboro. Juggling full-time work and family with my studies for four years wasn't easy, but I graduated with a Bachelor of Arts degree in business administration. I'd long thought about starting my own company, and my exposure to early large-scale computers at White Sands pointed me toward a technical career. As life would have it, though, I went into education. I taught at the high school and college levels, and I joined the National Guard in whichever state we lived in at any given time. I loved inspiring kids, especially disadvantaged youth who needed a loving but firm hand as they began to make their own way in an often tough and cruel world. But as difficult as the world can be at times, it is also full of joy and hope if you just allow yourself to see the good through the bad.

My family moved around a lot as I went from one teaching position to the next. My life with Willa and the kids was generally good, though, like any marriage, ours had its ups and downs. I think some of the downs resulted from the ghosts I continued to carry around from my childhood and from my combat experiences in Korea. Finally, Willa had had enough, and we got divorced in 1971.

For sixteen years after that, I remained single and focused on my own life and career. You might say I was something of a nomad. I even joined the Peace Corps in 1982 and taught at the University of Liberia for two years. I'd always wanted to live in Africa, the land of my ancestors, and I always wanted to help people less fortunate than I was. My time in the Peace Corps opened my eyes to what life was like for black people outside the United States. Life was difficult for American and Liberian blacks alike, though for entirely different reasons.

After I returned home from the Peace Corps, I started my own software design company, Smith Technologies. We did data processing for accounting procedures for private companies and universities in the Southwest. I'd managed to cobble together loans from the Small Business Association, federal grants, and enough capital from private individuals to launch the business. However, the economy was not good in the mid-1980s, and computers were still relatively new. They were nowhere near as common as they are now. The company didn't make it after five hard years of long hours, heartache, and indigestion. Losing my entrepreneurial dreams was hard for me.

The years of struggling with Smith Technologies did yield a blessing in January 1987. I was having dinner at a Quality Inn in Window Rock, Arizona, when I saw one of the most beautiful ladies I ever laid eyes on. I figured, *Oh, what the hell can you lose, Ed?* I sauntered over to her and gave her my business card. She must have liked me because she agreed to meet with me the next day. Louise was an Arizona native and a Cornell graduate. We hit it off right away, and we were married in April that same year. Having a woman in my life again turned me around in many ways, but I'm sad to say it wasn't enough.

My ghosts remained firmly entrenched. My dear wife left me in 2012, and I've not dated since that time. As I've said, I'm okay with that. I'm old. I'm happy with my life as it is, though I still sorely miss Louise. I even sometimes wonder if she'll come back one day. And lest you think inner ghosts and demons are just excuses for a guy to be difficult with those he loves, do please think again. You don't have to see combat or be abandoned by your parents to carry ghosts and demons with you that get in the way of love and relationships. Believe me—the offices of psychologists, psychiatrists, and therapists are full of people with ghosts and demons of their own. I think the trick is to come up with enough courage to admit you've got a problem and then come up with even more courage to deal with it. After Louise left, I went into serious therapy. I'm still in it. I'm happy to say that it helps a lot.

Over the years, my military trajectory continued to rise. As I said, I was always part of the National Guard in any state where I lived. Through the intercessions of some white generals, one of whom originally hailed from Pennsylvania, I was fast-tracked for a direct commission. I achieved the rank of major in 1978 and that of lieutenant colonel in 1986. It was still not easy for blacks to achieve high military ranks, but moving up the ladder was much easier than it had been in years past. An American soldier in the army is green, not white, black, brown, red, or yellow. Just olive-drab green. That's the way it should be, and I'm glad to see that is largely the case today.

After we went back to active duty, Fred and I drifted apart. We no longer were as close as we were while growing up and while fighting in King Company in Korea. I suppose that's natural and understandable. Great geographical distances separated us from that time on. I also think—no, I know—that Fred carried his own suitcase full of ghosts and demons. He died of a massive heart attack in 1996.

I continue on, as always. I have my faith, my kids, and my new and old friends. I have the quiet solitude and beauty of the Zuni Mountains, and I have a new dog!

Yes, life is good! It's very good indeed.

ACKNOWLEDGMENTS

No great thing ever gets done alone. The human experience is collaborative, tribal; a collective comes together to accomplish shared objectives. Yes, the writing process is by its very nature a solitary act, but what goes into the effort remains part of a larger tapestry. Thus, I owe a debt of gratitude to many individuals and organizations.

I wish to thank my six beautiful children for all the support they've shown me through the good times and the hard times. Without them, my life would mean little. You are all everything to me, and I am grateful to you for your love, caring, and tender support.

I offer thanks to my dearest friends of many, many years. You know who you are.

My thanks also go to the good people at the Veterans Administration, especially my therapist. In recent years, I've struggled to come to terms with my combat experiences. You can't do that alone. You need help, and I'm receiving it.

When I first began writing this book, I was at a complete loss as to how to proceed. I don't have a computer. I don't know how to type. I simply had many pages of handwritten text in a loose-leaf binder. Then I met a wonderful, intelligent young lady by the name of Jovanie Salcido. She's now a good friend. Thank you, Jovanie! You helped type the book's original draft, and you've helped me through the publishing process. I am forever grateful to you.

I would also like to thank the good people at Rushmore Press. They helped me through the publishing process from start to finish.

My ghostwriter, David W. Shaw, deserves special thanks. Without him, this book would never have seen the light of day.

And, last, I wish to thank all the men and women in the US military. Thank you for your valor, courage, endurance, and self-sacrifice. You are not forgotten.

ABOUT THE AUTHORS

EDWARD LEE SMITH SR. IS a retired lieutenant colonel, having served in the US Army and National Guard for more than two decades. An avid believer in the value of education, Smith has taught at the high school and college levels. As an educator, he was particularly dedicated to teaching disadvantaged youth. At eighty-nine, he's slowed down a bit, but he still gives motivational speeches that he hopes inspire others to be the best they can be. Smith holds a Bachelor of Arts degree in business administration from North Carolina Agricultural and Technical State University in Greensboro. He currently lives high up in the Zuni Mountains of New Mexico.

DAVID W. SHAW IS THE author of seven nonfiction books, including The Sea Shall Embrace Them. This riveting true story of the sea was an alternate selection of the Book-of-the-Month Club and was designated as one of the top-ten nonfiction books in 2002 by People magazine. Shaw is an award-winning journalist. He has published more than one thousand articles in a career that spans more than thirty years. His credits in periodicals include the New York Times, the Newark Star-Ledger, Reader's Digest, Woman's World, Entrepreneur, SAIL magazine, New Jersey Monthly, and many others.